NORTH-EAST
IN
BENTHIC ZONE

NORTH-EAST
IN
BENTHIC ZONE

DHANABIR LAISHRAM

AKANSHA PUBLISHING HOUSE
NEW DELHI-110002 (INDIA)

AKANSHA PUBLISHING HOUSE
4649-B/21, Ansari Road
Darya Ganj, New Delhi - 110 002
Ph.: 23263193/9811582579
Fax: 011-23263193
Email: ektabooks@yahoo.com

North-East in Benthic Zone

First Published 2007
ISBN–978–81–8370–114-3

[The responsibility for the facts stated, conclusions reached etc., is entirely that of the author. The publisher is not responsible for them, whatsoever.]

PRINTED IN INDIA

Published by **M.P. Misra** for **Akansha Publishing House**, New Delhi and Printed at Aryan Enterprises, Delhi.

For the next generation

DINESH AND DHANAPIYARI

DECOV and URMILA

and the next

THOI THOI

and

Ting Ting

PREFACE

Many writers have analogised the current impasse in the region of North-East India as 'in-flame'. Even the question of Benthic location (Deep Sea) comes up. The question is why? It would be futile exercise if one tries to answer it without taking the trouble of studying the political economy of the region. The problem of underdevelopment in NE has assumed a complex political and cultural form. Basically, in the parlance of political economy, development is related both to a prevalent mode of production as well as reproduction of social relations of production. Therefore, the political economy of underdevelopment takes into account the social relations of production and its genesis in a given system of production. The region being a cultural and economic periphery of India's mainland exhibits relationship of dependency between the modes of production prevalent in NE and the modes of production prevalent in the larger domain of India's economy. The vivid evidence for this dependency relation lies in the fact that NE acts as a supplier of raw material for the mainland and in turn serves as a market for finished goods from the mainland. This process of resource use could unite all the markets of India including NE but left the people divided. It leads to heterogeneous, overlapping and formalism in social and political aspects of the region. This relationship with the Indian capital does not ensure the self-determination of NE. Rather, it provides a space for operation of the Indian capital.

Such centre-states relationship seems to manifest India's power hegemony over the region in order to complete nation building processes which were coercive in nature. On the contrary the Indian capital gives rise to dominant ideology of subsumption of regional identities based on radical transformation of their societies. It shows that politically constructed identities resist the processes of dominance and homogenization. Such resistance is articulated as struggle for survival and sustenance. It is really antithesis of India's power hegemony. Even now, it is searching the historical importance and rights above of economic discontentment. In other words, in terms of "Political Economy" with the rise of dependency between NE and the mainland India, there has been a corresponding rise of resistance as its dialectical counterpart.

The corresponding rise of resistance to such hegemony is also fragmented. So the principle antagonistic contradiction could not be beyond the question. Moreover, economic dependency creates sub-peripheralization, i.e. peripheries within peripheries. Consequently, the values and the ideas which people hold about the nature of polity is completely based on relative deprivation without taking into account, the question of structural injustice. Such rational choices of major actors of NE compounded all the social and political fabric of the region. Here, one could assess that it may also be the form of contention.

Lastly, in the Benthic zone, i.e., the deepest part of the sea, the benthos in their struggle for survival have themselves evolved to have their own ray in order to find their survival needs in the dark which otherwise would have become extinct due to starvation. It is metaphorsied with the armed struggle in the region which rises its head as an antithesis borne out of the unequal and exploitative treatment to the northeasterners meted out by the mainstream coupled with the power hegemony of the later. But as attentive public and applied intellectuals, we are duty-bound to seek solutions to such vexed problems of the region. The present work is a modest attempt to anticipate some fresh thinking on the resilient insurrections for higher political status experiencing in the region. Lastly, any proposition for possible solution to the impasse calls for sacrifice from the part either of the dialectical counter parts. In this book an alternative paradigm to the genesis of all these problems are put forward for consideration.

DHANABIR LAISHRAM

Acknowledgements

In the making of this book, I have benefited immensely from the long-term interactions with my colleagues at AMUCO office and their support. I am grateful to my friends - Surjit Chongtham, Jagat Thoudam, Ito Tongbram, N.C. Khuman, Tompok Likmabam, R. Yangsosong Koireng, Dayananda, Tammi, Maisnam Bobo (Chinglen), Devan Sharma, Rajen, Subhas and Pabung Iboyaima. They have over the years helped me in grappling with the analytical politico-economic studies of the North-East India, often through a great deal of polemics and many heated discussions and disagreements.

A large number of young and aged colleagues – Sanatomba, Koireng, Amal, Gourachandra, Ibobi, Jasanta Kumar, Islam, Megha, S. Bhubon, K. Sopen, S. Sunilkanta, H. Dineshore, Hodam Gyaneshore, Kishan, Indrakumar and T. Tomba have contributed in evolving my ideas . Moreover, they have also assisted me in several other ways and have helped me in keeping my optimism alive.

I also express my sincere thanks to Prof. N. Joykumar, the Director of the Centre for Manipur Studies, Manipur University and his staff and my senior colleagues in the Department of Political Science, Manipur University for taking personal interest in my work. Views and suggestions shared by them have helped in improving the work from its previous draft.

Laishram Robel and Mr. Dinesh also shared a great deal of burden for type-setting the manuscript. I am also thankful to both of them for completing it at the least possible time.

As usual Prof. Naorem Sanajaoba, Gauhati University and Prof. Ksh. Bimola Devi have inspired me in multiple ways in writing this book. Without their inspiration, this book would not have seen the light of the day.

I am also thankful to Oza Thongam Yaiskul for taking the trouble of reading the whole manuscript and editing it to my utmost satisfaction.

Thanks are also due to Mr. Nobokishore and his organisation, Centre for Social Development (CSD) for their financial assistance.

However, I alone am responsible for the short-comings and omissions in my work.

DHANABIR LAISHRAM

CONTENTS

1

A BRIEF HISTORY OF NORTH-EAST INDIA

The states of North-East (NE) are late-comers into the mainstream of India. They are adjacent to various foreign countries such as Myanmar, Bangladesh, China, Bhutan and Nepal. In short 99 per cent of it is covered by international boundaries and the remaining one per cent is linked between NE and India at Siliguri, the chicken neck portion in the India's political map. The region is the composition of seven states constituted by Assam, Nagaland, Mizoram Manipur, Tripura, Meghalaya and Arunachal Pradesh.[1] Their combined population, according to the 2001 census, is 38.5 million and it represents 3.8 per cent of the total population of India. The total area of the region is 255,089 sq. km accounting for 8.05 per cent of the country's total area. The states along with their capitals and its areas (in sq. km) and languages are given in the table below:

Sl. No.	State	Capital	Area in sq. km	Major speaking languages
1.	Assam	Dispur	78,438	Assamese, Bengali Bodo, Karbi, Rabha, Dimasa
2.	Arunachal Pradesh	Itanagar	83,743	Monpa, Aka, Nishi
3.	Nagaland	Kohima	16,579	Aao, Konyak, Sema, Angami
4.	Manipur	Imphal	22,327	Manipuri
5.	Mizoram	Aizwal	21,087	Mizo
6.	Tripura	Agartala	10,486	Tripuri, Bengali
7.	Meghalaya	Shillong	22,429	Khasi, Garo

The so-called seven sister states of North-East constitute this family of "enchanted frontiers". As varied and different as the states are from each other, yet there is also a lot of similarity and common feature in their origin, stage of civilization, food habit, ancient customs and these beautiful land, best describe the North-East.

Assam is bounded by Bhutan and Arunachal in the north; Nagaland and Manipur in the east; Bangladesh, Meghalaya, Tripura and Mizoram in the South. The land of Assam consists of valleys and hills and mighty rivers like the Brahmaputra and Barak. Assam has a geographical area of 78,438 sq. km about 26,638,407 people comprising of 13,787,799 males and 12,850,608 females (2001 Census). The literacy rate stands at 64.28 per cent. The principal language of Assam is Assamese although a large number of other languages are spoken such as Bodo, Karbi, Rabha and Dimasa. Except for a narrow corridor running through the foothills of the Himalayas that connects the state with West Bengal, Assam is almost entirely isolated from India. The capital of Assam is Dispur, a suburb of Guwahati.

The name "Assam" is derived from the term "Axom" which, in Sanskirit, refers to unequal or unrivalled. The uneven topography of the land, full of hills, plains and rivers might, therefore, have contributed to her name. The Mongolian Ahom dynasty, which had ruled Assam for more than six hundred years, might also be the cause for her name. Assam is a land with an illustrious recorded history going back to the 4th century BC. Assam was an independent kingdom throughout all of history till the end of the first quarter of the 19th century when the British conquered the Kingdom and annexed it to British India.

Assam is an agricultural state. Agriculture accounts for the livelihood of about four-fifths of its people in

Assam. The principal food crop is rice. Cash crops such as jute, tea, cotton, oilseeds and sugarcane are also grown. It is also known for her forest wealth with varieties of flora and fauna.

Assam has two important physical regions – the Barak valley and the Brahmuptra valley. The state is characterized by heavy rainfall varying between 178 and 305 cm., usually during the months from June to September every year. Thus, it suffers from both floods and landslide. It has a total area of 78,438 sq.km and one-fourth of which is forest area. It is divided into 23 districts. The total population of the state is 2.66 crores as per 2001 census. The density of population is 340 persons per sq.km., the highest in the North-Eastern Region. The state has 37,652 schools.

The natural resources of the state include rich mineral wealth like coal, limestone, refractory clay, dolomite and natural gas. Petroleum and petroleum products, tea and natural gases generate considerable revenues for India.

Assam is famous for producing 15.6 per cent of the world's tea and 55 per cent of India's tea production in about 750 tea plantations. Other industries include fertilizers, sugar, jute, silk, paper, plywood, rice mills and oil drilling and a number of cottage industries including handloom, sericulture, bamboo and cane and brass utensils have also come up in the state. The per capita income in 1998-99 at 1993-94 prices was Rs.5587, which is quite low among the North Eastern states.[2]

To the southeast of Assam lies the equally enchanted state of Manipur, a land of vitality and sports which possess rich martial culture and tradition. The game of polo is accepted world wide to have been conceived out of the mud of the state. The state is of unique distinction for having the Meetei Vaishnavites, the Meeteis Sanamahi, Meetei Pangal, along with the ethnically distinctive 33 recognised scheduled tribes and many other in the category of unspecified list. These ethnic tribes are categorized into two groups known as Manipuri Nagas and Manipuri Kukis. No doubt, there are non-Naga or non-Kuki tribes.

Manipur, literally meaning "A Jeweled land" nestle deep within a lush green corner of North East India. It seems much like an exquisite work of art executed by superb hands of nature and is indeed a state of exquisite natural beauty and splendour, the beauty of which once inspired Mrs. St. Clair Grimwood describes it as "A Pretty Place more beautiful than many show places of the world". The terrain in the state is predominantly hilly, except a broad central valley extending to about 1800 sq. km. The average altitude of the hilly region is upto 3,000m. The Imphal and the Barak rivers flowing in southern direction form the main drainage system.

Manipur has Nagaland to its north, Mizoram to its south, upper Myanmar to its east, and Cachar district of Assam to its west. The total area of the state is 22,327 sq. km out of which more than 27 per cent constitutes forests. The total population of the state is 23.88 lakh–12.07 lakh males and 11.81 lakh females. The rate of growth of population during 1991-2001 was 30.02 per cent. The literacy rate of the state (2001 census) was 68.87 percent, with female literacy of 59.70 per cent and male literacy of 77.87 per cent. The sex ratio in the state is 978 females per 1000 males. The population density is 107 per sq.km.

The per capita income in the state in 1998-99 at 1993-94 prices was only Rs.7132. The state thus shows a contrast in its literacy status and sex ratio which are better than the national average while it has a very low utilization of human resources.[3]

Manipur became a union territory in 1956 and a full-fledged state in 1972. It has nine districts. The handloom industry is the biggest employer in the state with more than three lakh persons employed at its three lakh spindles. The 5970 small-scale industrial units provide employment to about 24,000 workers. The silk industries (Tassar Silk) has considerable potential in providing employment to the state's population in its various stages, including mulberry-raising.[4]

Little is known about the early history of what is now Nagaland, including the origin of several large sandstone pillars at Dimapur. The British rule was established over the area by the 1890s, and head-hunting, then a traditional practice, was outlawed. The Naga territory remained split between Assam and the North East Frontier Agency (NEFA). After Indian independence in 1947, despite a vocal movement advocating the political union of all the Naga tribes; one faction called for sovereignty. In 1957, following violent incidents, the Indian government established a single Naga administrative unit under Indian rule. In 1960, the Indian government agreed to make Nagaland a self-governing state within India. The state of Nagaland was formally inaugurated on 1st December, 1963, as the 16th State of the Indian Union.

Nagaland has Myanmar to its east, Manipur to its south, Assam to its west and north, and Arunachal Pradesh to its north-east. It has a total area of 16,579 sq.km out of which more than half of it is covered by forests. It has a population density of 120 persons per sq.km. The total population of 19.88 lakh comprises 10.4 lakh males and 9.5 lakh females. The population has grown by 64.4 per cent in the decade prior to 2001. The sex ratio is 909 females to 1000 males. The literacy rate in the state is 67.1 per cent with male literacy of 72.0 per cent and female literacy of 62.0 per cent. Nagaland has eight districts where enhanced terraced cultivation, farm forestry, crechard plantation, and case crops plantation are done as livelihood means. A number of agro- and forest-based industries has come up in the state. It has a low per capita income of Rs.10,287 (in 1997-98 at 1993-94 prices).[5]

Nagaland, though tiny in its territory, has pride of its numerous warrior tribes, who tax independence more valuable than life. A distinctive feature of the people is their racial homogeneity, despite a wide diversity with respect to tongue and tradition, and as sheltered under the Naga umbrella.

Mizoram is bordering Myanmar in the East and South and Bangladesh in the West. The terrain is hilly and mostly undulating with average altitude ranging from 500 to 800 m and maximum reaching 2,157 m in Blue Mountains. The Chhimtuipui is the only major river. Aizwal is its capital. The average rainfall is 2500 mm.

Perching on the high hills of North-eastern corner, Mizoram is a storehouse of natural beauty hills its endless variety of landscape, hilly, terrains, meandering streams, deep gorges, rich wealth of flora and fauna.

Mizoram is a mountainous region which became the 23rd state of the Union in February 1987. It was one of the districts of Assam till 1972 when it became Union

Territory. Flanked by Bangladesh on the west and Myanmar on the east and south, Mizoram occupies an important strategic position having a long international boundary of 722 km with Myanmar and Bangladesh. Mizoram has the most variegated hilly terrain in the eastern part of India. The hills are steep and are separated by rivers which flow either to the north or the south creating deep gorges between the hill ranges. The average height of the hills is about 900 metres. The highest peak in Mizoram is the Phawngpui (Blue Mountain) with a height of 2210 metres. Mizoram has a pleasant climate. It is generally cool in summer and not very cold in the winter. Mizoram has great natural beauty and an endless variety of landscape and is very rich in flora and fauna. Almost all kinds of tropical trees and plants thrive in Mizoram. The hills are marvelously green. Mizos are closely knit society with no class distinction and no discrimination on ground of sex. The entire society is knit together by a peculiar code of ethics "Tlawmngaihna' implying to be hospitable kind, unselfish and helpful to others from each one.

Historians believe that the Mizos are a part of the great wave of the Mongolian race spilling over into the eastern and southern India centuries ago. The sojourn in Western Burma, into which they eventually went around the seventh century, is estimated to last about two centuries. They came under the influence of the British Missionaries in the 9th century, and now most of the Mizos are Christians. One of the beneficial result of Missionary activities was the spread of education. The Missionaries introduced the Roman script for the Mizo language and formal education. The cumulative result literacy rate is as high as 95 percentage which is considered to be highest in India. The Mizos are a distinct community and the social unit is the village. Around it revolves the life of a Mizo. Mizo village is usually set on the top of a hill with the chief's house at the centre and the bachelor's dormitory called *Zawlbuk*, prominently. In a way the focal point in the village was the *Zawlbuk* where all young bachelors of the village slept. *Zawlbuk* was the training ground and indeed, the cradle wherein the Mizo youth was shaped into a responsible adult member of the society.

Mizoram has a total area of 21,087 sq.km of which 61.72 per cent is covered by forests. It has a population of 3.9 lakh - 4.6 lakh males and the 4.3 lakh females. The population in the state grew during 1991-2001 by 29.18 per cent. The sex ratio is 924 females to 1000 males. It has a high literacy rate of 88.5 per cent with male literacy of 90.7 per cent and female literacy of 86.13 per centre. Its population density is 42 persons per sq.km.[6]

Mizoram became a full-fledged state in 1987. It is divided into three districts, and sub-divisions, with three autonomous hill district councils. There are altogether six towns and 301 village councils. The per capita income in the state in 1990-91 at current prices was Rs., 4451. Handloom and handicrafts constitute few major industrial activities and industries such as ginger, beverages, edible oil, and fruits preservation are growing rapidly.

Tripura is surrounded by Bangladesh on all sides excepting the narrow portion in the North-East which borders Assam and Mizoram. It has a total area of 10,486 sq.km of which nearly 60 per cent is covered by forests. The state has a total population of 31.4 lakh with 16.3 lakh males and 15.6 lakh females. The population grew by 15.7 per cent over a period of 10 years before 2001. It has a sex ratio of 950 females to 1000 males. The density of population is 304 per sq. km next to Assam in the entire north-eastern region.[7]

The literacy rate in Tripura is 73.7 per cent with 81.5 per cent male literacy rate and 65.4 per cent female literacy. The state administration is divided into four districts, ten administrative sub-divisions, 177 tehsils and 5215 villages. It has 49 tea gardens covering an area of 55.27 lakh hectares. Handloom constitutes the major industrial activity in the state. There is a network of primary weavers' co-operative societies supported by an Apex society. The per capita income of the state is only Rs. 6,214 (in 1998-99 at 1993-94 prices).[8]

In olden days, Tripura was a proud kingdom ruled by a succession of 183 Tripuri Prince who held sway over a land whose history is etched over centuries in the *Rajmala*, the state chronicle. On the eve of partition, a part of Tripura plain was inhabited by Muslims, though the overall demographic position was over-whelming Tripuri nationality. With the creation of East Pakistan, Tripura was virtually isolated. Tripura merged with India on 15th October,1949, and she became a Part C state with the inauguration of the new Constitution on 26th January, 1950 and subsequently a union territory in November 1956, attaining statehood only in January 1972.

With the influx of refugees from Bangladesh, migration was running at the rate of 10,000 a month.[9] The inexorable pressures of the migrant population soon found themselves being pushed into less hospital lands in the hilly interiors. In short, the indigenous people are Tripura nationality, who recently have found themselves outnumbered by refugee Bengalis who have become the dominant majority and have taken over the running of the state.

The state of Arunachal Pradesh is located in North-east India and comprises an area of 83,743 sq.km. Itanagar is the capital of Arunachal Pradesh. Arunachal Pradesh which is separated from Tibet by the Himalayan range stretching over 600 kilometres along the mountain range from east to west. The proportions of the state reinforced the argument for an additional time zone. With spectacular Himalayan views it has numerous famous planes like the Bomdi La and the Nathu La, providing assessing routes to neighbouring Bhutan and massive China. Even today China claims the state as disputed land with India. Its people present a fascinating mix of Tibeto-Burmese origin with about fifty different dialects. This state is regarded as the most peaceful place in the region, with Mizoram and Meghalaya running close to second and the third.

The state has 13 districts, and a substantial part of it is covered by mountains except for thin strips of land, most part of which adjoin Assam. More than two-thirds of the total area is forest; Scheduled Tribes (STs) constitute 79 per cent of its populations. As per the 2001 census, the state has a total population of 10.96 lakh; 5.79 lakh males and 5.17 lakh females. The population grew by 26.21 per cent during 1991-2001. The sex ratio is 901 females to 1000 males. The literacy rate is 54.74 per cent – the male literacy rate in 64.07 and the female literacy rate is only 44.24 per cent. The per capita income of the state by 1998-99 estimated at 1993-94 prices was Rs. 8,001. The density of population in the state is 13 persons per sq.km which is the lowest in the entire North-Eastern Region. Arunachal Pradesh was accorded the status of a union territory on 20 January 1972 and that of a state on 20th February 1987.

The state holds considerable potential in hydel power. More than 80 per cent of its population is, however, engaged in agriculture, especially in jhumming or shifting cultivation. Crops are raised by clearing forests and are usually sown one to three times a year, depending on the fertility of the soil. The main crops are rice, maize, millet, wheat, and mustard. There is a potential for significant growth of forest-based industries including saw mills, ply-wood and veneer mills, rice mills, fruit preservation units, oil expellers, and so on. Handloom and handicrafts industry is another area where the state holds considerable revenue and employment potential. Since 1992, the tourism industry has registered impressive growth.

It would be noteworthy to note that the state lags behind the national average in terms of literacy level for both males and females, sex ratio, per capita income, and many other parameters. The pattern of distribution of workers across diverse work sectors indicates that more than 80 per cent of the workforce is still confined to the primary sector, and agriculture.[10]

In Arunachal Pradesh, the people may be broadly divided into three cultural groups on the basis of their socio-religious affinities. The Monpas and Sherdukpens of Tawang and Weast Kameng districts follow the Lamaistic tradition of Mahayana Buddhiusm. Noted for their religious fervour, their villages have richly decorated Buddhist temples, locally called *Gompas*. Though largely agriculturists practising terrace cultivation, many of these people are also pastoral and breed herds of yak and mountain sheep. Culturally similar to them are Membas and Khambas who live in the high mountains along the northern borders.

Khamptis and Singphos inhabiting the eastern part of the state are Buddists. They are said to have migrated from Thailand and Burma long ago and their ancient scripts brought from their original homeland are still in use.

The second group of people are Adis, Akas, Apatanis, Bangnis, Nishis, Mishmis, Mijis, Thongsas etc., who worship Sun and Moon God namely. Donyi-Polo and Abo-Tani, the original ancestors for most of these tribes. Their religious rituals, largely coincide with phases of agricultural cycles. They invoke nature deities and make animal sacrifices. They traditionally practise jhumming or shifting cultivation. Adis and Apatanis extensively practise rice cultivation and have an agricultural economy. Apatanis are famous for their paddy-cum-pisciculture. They are specialised over centuries in harvesting two crops of fish along with each crop of paddy.

The third group comprises Noctes and Wanchos, adjoining Nagaland in the Tirap District. They are hardly people known for their strictly structured village society in which hereditary village chief still plays a vital role. The Noctes also practise an elementary form of Vaishnavism.

The state of Meghalaya is situated on the north-east of India. It extends for about 300 km in length and about 100 km in breadth. It is bounded on the north by Goalpara, Kamrup and Nowgong districts, on the east by Karbi Anglong and North Cachar Hills districts, all of Assam, and on the south and west by Bangladesh. Shillong, the capital of Meghalaya is located at an altitude of 1496 metres above sea level.

Emergence of Meghalaya as an autonomous state on 2nd April 1970 and as a full-fledged state on 21st January 1972 marked the beginning of a new era of the geo-political history of North-eastern India. Shillong, which was made Assam's capital in 1874, remained so till January 1972, following the formation of Meghalaya. The capital city derives its name from the manifestation of the creator called Shillong.

Meghalaya is the homeland, mainly, of the Khasis, the Jaintias and the Garos. The Garos inhabit western Meghalaya, the Khasis in central Meghalaya, and the Jaintias in eastern Meghalaya. The Khasi, Jaintia, Bhoi, War, collectively known as the Hynniewtrep people predominantly inhabit the districts of east of Meghalaya, also known to be one of the earliest ethnic group of settlers in this region, belonging to the Proto-Austroloid Monkhmer race. The Garo Hills is predominantly inhabited by the Garos, belonging to the Bodo family of the Tibeto-Burman race, said to have migrated from Tibet. The Garos call themselves Achik-manda. In the Garo language *Achik* means Hills and *mands* meaning man. So, Achik-mande means the Hills people.

The Khasis inhabit the eastern part of Meghalaya, in the Khasi and Jaintia Hills. The Khasis residing in Jaintia hills are now better known as Jaintias. They are also called Pnars. The Khasis occupying the northern lowlands and foothills are generally called Bhois. Those who live in the southern tracts are termed Wars.

Again among the wars, those living in the Khasi are called War-Khasis and those in the Jaintia Hills, War-Pnars or War-Jaintias. In the Jaintia Hills Khyrwangs, Labangs, Nangphllutes, Nangtungs inhabit in the northeastern part and in the east. In the Khasi Hills the Lyngngams live in the north western part. But all of them claim to have descended from the 'Ki Hynniw Trep' and are now known by the generic name of Khasi-Pnars or simply Khasis. They have the same traditions, customs and usages with a little variation owing to geographical divisions.[11]

Meghalaya, which literally means 'Abode of the Clouds', more than lives up to its reputation – a land of scenic beauty with waterfalls, rivulets, hills and takes in the heart of Shillong. This was the erstwhile British capital of undivided Assam, educational nucleus and seat of government for the entire province up to 1970, when the state was formed. Meghalaya's distinctive tribes – Khasi, Jaintia and Garo are some of the few remaining matrilineal societies in the world. A democratic way of life and rules of democratic propriety are features that have been handed down through the ages. The people are jovial, with a rare absence of institutional caste barriers and an accepted equality of the sexes.

Meghalaya has total area of 22,429 sq.km. of which 46.24 per cent is covered by forests. The total population of 23.06 lakh includes 11.67 lakh male and 11.38 lakh female. The population grew by 29.94 per cent in the decade 1991-2001. It has a sex ratio of 975 females per 1000 males. The literacy rate as per 2001 census was 63.31 per cent, the male literacy rate 66.14 per cent and female literacy rate is 60.41 per cent.[12]

The state is shown at a higher level than the national average in terms of sex ratio and female literacy rates. However, it lags behind in terms of overall literacy and male literacy: the population growth rate is also higher than the national rate during the correspondent period. Another area of concern is the low per capita income of

Rs.7,606 in 1998-99 at 1993-94 prices. Agriculture is the primary source of income for the workers in the five districts in the state. The state has launched a jhum control scheme to encourage the people to undertake cultivation on improved land through the supply of fertilizers, seeds, irrigation, and other facilities. The industrial base in the state is beginning to grow with industries such as ply wood edible oil, limestone, mining and cement.

These are the face values of all these seven states, in reality many are frustrated and helpless in the face of pressures similar to those in other parts of the fourth world.[13] Drugs and Alcohol are major concerns as having right to euthanaia.[14] The lack of development in the whole state, due in part to its geographic isolation, government's long term negligence and the influx of population from neighbouring countries is increasing cases of violence and unrest. Ethnic differences are being emphasised more and more as competition for jobs, trade, and rights increases. Besides, step motherly treatment of union government breed many insurgency groups and showing political aspiration of self-determination. But some are external self-determination and some are at stake for internal self-determination.[15] That means emerging of internal contradiction can be seen. The question is why? The answer should be given after analyzing the history of British colonialism and India's democratic political system towards the states of NE India. So, it is better to see the territorial development of NE with the two external forces of British and India in the past and present political processs.

Territorial Administrative Complexes

The three valleys surrounded by blue mountain ranges constitute the sensitive region known as northeastern India. The blue hills comprised by the eastern Himalayas on the north, the Naga and Manipur hills on the east, the Mizo and Tripura hills on the south and the Shillong plateau (named in the thirties by the Indian geographer, S.P. Chatterji, as Meghalaya) on the west, form almost completely natural boundaries of the Brahmaputra valley, the heartland of Assam. The district of Cachar is lying beyond the Shillong plateau. Between the naga hills (of Nagaland) and the chin hills(of Burma) is situated in the Manipur valley with an altitude of about 3000 ft.

The changes in NE India whether in the direction of positive or negative, constructive or destructive, these were caused by the external forces as well as the existing geographical factors. In the conventional form, location was critical to the development of administrative forms in the region. The formidable Himalayan ranges in the north and the east; gradual undulating Brahmaputra plains; and the plateaus and isolated hills in the south and west, all played a significant role. The former provided adequate barriers against invasions from the north and east. While the later provided strategic defensive positions, the region developed in isolation.[16]

The southern and western boundaries of the region were prone to invasions, as they permitted easy access. In fact, the region became receptive as waves of population groups gradually settled down. Invasional/ migrations and resultant territorial adjustments continued well up to the first half of the nineteenth century.

'The province of Assam at the far northeastern corner of India is a museum of nationalities', wrote J.B. Fuller in 1909.[17] Of these, the Garos living in the western part of the Meghalaya plateau have a legend of having migrated from the northwest, that is, the southern side of central Tibet.[18] The Khasi, at least some of them, claim to have migrated from Southeast Asia, part of their route probably passing through Burma.[19] The Kuki and the Chin inhabiting the southern hills of Manipur, Tripura and most of the Mizo hills are supposed to be from Southern China.[20] They are also believed to have contributed to the basic linguistic strain of the Meetei who inhabit the Manipur valley.[21] The Naga, settled in Nagaland and the northern hills of Manipur, and some of the groups in the northeast frontier are mostly assumed to be immigrants from eastern Tibet, whereas most of the inhabitants of the "sub-Himalayan and cis-Himalayan" areas trace their origin directly from Southern Tibet.[22]

When the Lushai tribes (the Mizos) eventually displaced the Kukis and others from the present-day Mizoram in the 1840s. This was besides the impact of the immigrants, who moved into the region with the British annexation of the area in 1826. These elements with different points of entry and time produced a complicated mix of population content. In a sense, the region was balkanized and exhibited homogeneity amidst heterogeneity.

The resultant dichotomy introduced by the internal territorial distinctions between the population groups proved to be tenacious in the accentuated micro differences. With expanding administrative influences, there emerged distinct contradictions in spatial organisation of space. This did not relate itself to the geographical phenomena. These distinctions later proved to be politically meaningful.

Evolution of the Region

A miniature replica of the country, the region maintained international and national contact through the Brahmaputra valley and the Cachar plains. These were reinforced by territorial and topographical distinctions that were channelised to repel and resist invasions; thereby, the fortunes of the hills and plains were inextricably woven together.

The region was broadly divided into the Brahmaputra and the Barak valleys along with Cachar, Manipur, Tripura, Garo, Khasi and Jaintia hills. North Cachar-Mikir-Mizo hills and parts of the North East Frontier Agency were also included. At times, the region extended well up to North Bengal and East Bengal up to the sea. The region at the beginning of the nineteenth century had an area of approximately 60,000 sq.km. and included all the dependencies and conquered territories in or beyond the mountainous limits that surrounded the Brahmaptura valley in every direction. This area was divided to represent 'Uttarakhol' – the northern bank territories, 'Dakhanikhol' or the south bank territories and the island of Majuli. Besides it was also divided on east west basis, with Kaliabor as the dividing point between the lower and upper Brahmaputra valley. This aspect is important because, upper Brahmaputra valley became the core of the various powers that later went on to carve out an empire in the region. This historical instance was reinforced by the British, who found in the area, factors conducive to further their strategic and commercial interests. As a result, this section dominated by Dibrugarh-Tinsukia axis even today retains its importance in the very fact of regional economic activities.[23]

This suggested that there was a definite pattern of movement-displacement control-decline process. These reflected the changing perception of space and the possible roles of the disruptive elements in the region's human geography. Through these super- impositions, the process of territorial alignment and fixation were slow, these were in place by the time of British annexation of the region in 1826.[24]

The movement into the region was from the north and north-east and at times from the south-eastern corners of the region. These were opposite to the developments that gradually penetrated the region from the south-west and west. Yet, one can clearly identify the pattern of territorial adjustment that has taken place in the region to largely compromise:

i) The Cacharis and the Ahoms along with the Bodos in the Brahmaputra valley;

ii) The Tibeto-Burman group along with the peripheral mountain systems; and

iii) The Mon-Khmer groups south of the valley.

It can also be added here that continuous pressure exerted by the successive waves of migrants into the region forced the previous inhabitants to move into the mountain vastness adjacent to the valley. Here, in the inaccessible and isolated terrain, these populations perpetuated their traditional socio-political transactions. Later, after 1826, these were reinforced by administrative measures. This duality in policy frameworks is evident even today. This became the trend setter that led to the fragmentation of the geographical entity that was the North-East.[25]

Territorial Development

Before the advent of the Ahoms in the early part of the thirteenth century, the region was shared by –

1. The Bodo-Shan groups of Chutiyas, east of Subansiri and Dihing rivers;
2. Bodo-Shan related groups controlling the areas south of (1);
3. The Kacheri kingdom to the west of 1 and 2 included parts of the present day Sibsagar and eastern Nagaon districts of Assam;
4. West of the Kacheri kingdom was the land of the Bhujias;
5. West of the Bhujia country and the rest was the kingdom of Kamrupa river in its western boundary.

Ahom belonging to the Tai group entered the region from the passes across the Himalaya in the north-eastern parts.[26] They crossed the Patkai range and established themselves in the south-eastern corner of upper Brahmaptura plains (in the area around present day Sibsagar district). In the subsequent three centuries, they displaced the Morans, the Borahis, the Nagas and the original inhabitants of the valley. In the process, they were able to extend effective control over Brahmaputra valley and a nominal control over the adjacent hill territories. In the later half of the seventeenth century, they came into open confrontation with the Mughal India. This enabled them to extend effective control over the lower Brahmaptura valley. The Ahoms control the area through series of forts and trading system. These networks became the carriers of socio-economic and political penetration in different corners of the region. Religo-cultural structure was dominated by feudalism which also supplied necessary man power at the time of war. These aspects took firmer roots with vernacularisation. On the whole, the Ahom power was based on agriculture and its stability depended on the valley. It encouraged the growth of sub-regional power centres.

The decline of the Ahoms coincided with the emergence of Manipur and Upper Burma as rival contending centers. The Singpos along with the Patkai range wrested control of the area east of river Burhi Dihing in 1794. Likewise the Khamptis established themselves along with the river Tegapani and extended their control over the frontier tracts along Sadiya.

Burmese interest in the region increased with the annexation of eastern and southern parts in 1762. They made their intentions clear with the intervention in the internecine struggle of the Ahoms as well as through their footholds in East Bengal. Part of the frontier mountain inhabitants joined the Burmese. As a consequence of the intervention, many Ahom areas were subjected to wholesale depopulation, collapse of agricultural and industrial bases and general neglect. This coincided with British intervention in 1823.

David Scott, the energetic frontier man of the East India Company, was appointed judge and magistrate of Rangpur, the northeastern district of Bengal in December 1812. In 1813, the company lost its monopoly over Indian trade. A greater trading contact with China, provided by the Sea of Canton, became an imperative necessity. The search for additional trade in Assam was a part of this need. The Gurkha war of 1814-16 opened western Tibet through the acquisition of new territories to the west of

Nepal, and the emphasis on Bhuttan for a route to Tibet was weakened for a while. But the eastward expansion continued. In September 1816, Scott was appointed as the Governor-General's Agent to the North-East Frontier in addition to his post as joint magistrate of Rangpur and commissioner of Cooch Behar, with the duty of exercising a general control and superintendence over political relations and intercourse with the petty states in that quarters' including Sikkim, Bhutan, Tibet, Cooch Behar, Bijni, Assam, Cachar, Manipur and Jaintia.[27]

While Scott was engaged in bringing the cotton producing Garos under British authority, a great opportunity opened up in Assam and Manipur with the beginning of internecine conflicts in the royal families of Assam and Manipur. Burmese intervention in these conflicts, and the worsening of Anglo-Burmese relations. The military defeat of Burma and the signing of the Treaty of Yandabo in 1826 led to the renunciation of Burmese claims on the territories of Assam and its dependencies and also with the contiguous petty states of Cachar and Jyntea. According to the official British interpretation, the Assam hills west of Patkoi range of mountains came under British possession by virtue of the treaty.[28] In 1852 lower Burma was annexed. In 1862 the ceded territories of Burma were constituted into a chief commissioners province. On 1 January 1886, upper Burma was annexed to it.[29]

In 1826, David Scott was appointed as senior commissioner of Assam in addition to his existing role. A Junior Commissioner was posted for upper Assam. Scott's advice for restoration of upper Assam to a subordinate monarchy, with a view to pacifying the Assamese gentry, was accepted by the Supreme

Government after a series of revolts had taken place and the position of the East India Company had become shaky in England. In 1833, Prince Purandar Singh was installed but was replaced in 1838 on a vague charge of 'mal-administration'. In 1842, Sadiya and the Mutlock territory (Dibrugarh) also were annexed, extending direct British rule over the entire Brahmaputra valley. The Cachar plain was annexed in 1832 and its northern hills in two instalments, in 1839 and 1854. Manipur, however, was not annexed.

In the wake of the Burmese attack, the British extended 'protection' to the Jaintia King and secured, from the siem (chief) of Nongkhlow, Tirot Singh, permission for the construction of a sanatorium and a road from Sylhet to Kamrup through his territory. But later Tirot Singh grew suspicious of the British intention. He was joined in his resistance to the penetration by some other Khasi Chiefs in 1829, but was crushed in 1829, two years after Scott's death. The Khasi chiefs had to enter into subordinate alliances with the British government and in all surrendered 31 villages to the British. In 1835, the Jaintia king was removed and his territory merged with British India. The Khashi chiefship were reduced to 25 in number under four kinds of chiefs' siem, wahadadar, sirdar and lyngdoh.[30]

Once the organised states in the region were brought under British control, the subordination of the turbulent hill people was a matter of time. Cotton, minerals, wild rubber and wild tea held out prospects for profit from the hills. Shortly after 1826, exploration for coal started in Assam. Though petroleum was discovered, it was not until 1865 that experimental drilling was initiated (shortly after that, Assam became a chief commissioner's province). Tea received the most immediate attention. By 1830, uncertainty appeared in the East India Company's trade with China, the supplier of indigenous tea was reported from the Singpho area, and during the Anglo-Burmese war a Scottish soldier, Robert Bruce, learnt its preparation from Singpho Chief, tea plantation was planned only after the annexation of upper Assam in 1838. Meanwhile, a bid to import tea seeds from China was unsuccessful but a few Chinese plantation workers who reached Assam were employed under Charles Bruce, brother of Robert Bruce to develop tea plants. In 1838, Assam tea was opened for private competition and Bruce was sacked.[31] The spread of the tea gardens from the middle of the nineteenth century strengthened the case for a 'forward policy' on the hills.

With this consolidation, activities were concentrated to bring the inhabitants of the mountain sections under active administration. Area below the Paktai range, inhabited by Singhpos, Khamptis, Mihirs, eastern Nagas and others was incorporated in 1843.[32] The Rengma Nagas and the Mihirs occupying the tract south of Naogong and west of Patkai were brought under control between 1838 and 1848. In 1866, the Angami country along with the watershed area of river Doyang was annexed. The headquarters was re-located at Samguting. In 1879, the district headquarters was moved to Kohima. By 1889, the entire Aao Naga country was brought under British administration! Lastly in 1890, British conquered Manipur after having a big war at Khongjom. It was known to the Manipuris, as "the war of independence of Manipur". The Manipuris fought against the British for a good number of days in four battlefields. In this war, many British officers were killed. But the powerful British conquered Manipur after defeating Paona Major

General and his soldiers in the battlefield of Khongjom on 23rd April 1891.[33]

Thus, the British with active forward policy from 1839 onwards, were able to establish their control over the area. To a large extent in the initial stages they followed the Ahom administrative pattern. Administration was extended in planned phases with frequent resource to the existing systems. However, by 1863, in order to have better supervisory control, the administrative headquarters of this province was shifted from Rangpur and Cachar to Cherrapunji and Shillong. In 1873, Inner Line policy was introduced, and with the exception of the Garo, the Khaši and the Jaintia hills, all other units were brought under its preview.

It is necessary to note that until the British advent, the notion of territorial or political authority was unknown in the hills. Thus, the frontier between the sub-Himalayan and cis-Himalayan British territory and Tibet was fixed only with the drawing of the Mc Mahon Line in 1914. To the south of the Surma valley, the Chin-Lushai hills, 'a tract of most intricate hill ranges and impenetrable cane-brakes' was terra incognita before 1839.[34] Premberton reported that the Lushai country east of Tripura had once been under the control of the ruler of Tripura.[35] But Mackenzie held that Tripura's authority over the Lushai had never been settled or absolute.[36] Probably, depending upon the feuds, the fluctuating strength and the mobility of the hill people, the rulers of Tripura, Cachar, Manipur and Burma controlled parts of the region from time to time. Consequently, the British advance on the hills was from all these sides. In 1777, for the first time a friendly Chief in the Chittangong Hill Tract sought British assistance against Kuki raids. Successive raids on the gardens, and punitive measures since 1869 led to the Lushai expeditions of 1871-72 and 1889 after which the hills were brought under rule.

Formation of Political Organisation

Consequent to annexation and consolidation of the region (1826) colonial administrators made constant territorial readjustments, so much so that from 1826 to 1873, Assam became a part of Bengal. With the addition of the districts of Goalpara, Sylhet and Cachar, it became a separate province in 1874. All the new territories inhabited by the intermediary tribes were in stages included in the province, like that of the present day Nagaland, Mizoram etc. or were brought under the purview of the native rulers like those of Manipur who administered the areas occupied by the western Naga tribes for the colonial administrators. However, under the Curzon Plan of partition of Bengal Province, Assam and adjacent territories were once again brought under common nomenclature of East Bengal and Assam Province. Later, with its annulment, the region got its own independent administrative identity in 1912.[37]

Be that as it may be, these changes resulted in the region comprising of-

a) Assam with the districts of Goalpara, Kamrup, Nagaon, Darrang, Sibsagar, and Lakhimpur, the Barak-Surma valley(Sylhet and Cachar Districts); the Khasi the Jaintia the Naga and the Lushai hill districts,

b) The native kingdoms of Manipur and Tripura; and

c) The North Eastern frontier Tracts or the present day state of Arunachal Pradesh governed by the administrative head of the province for the centre.

This process of territorial adjustments over time and space, gave the region its unique characteristics of heterogeneity. This later aspect extended its influences on various regional activities in the form of variation in socio-political and economic representation and participation of the population groups and sub-groups. To this complex milieu, the influx of population from the Gangetic delta complicated the inter-group relations in the region. Very much different from other areas of NE India, in Manipur, a good number of notable movements were launched by the people against the feudalism and colonial administration of the British. They were Women Agitation I (1904), Thoubal Lal in 1912, Kuki Rebellion 1917 to 1919, Zadonang movement from 1921 to 1929, Irawat Movement from 1932 to 1951 and Women Agitation II of 1939.[38]

Post-partition developments saw the expressed fear of the inhabitants of the North East region of absorption and dominance. Large-scale influx of immigrants and dominance of regional activity by the plain inhabitants reinforced this. This resulted in the accentuation of the ideological and political differences within the region. Moreover, some of the policies, such as the language bill, were responsible in alienating the different population groups from each other.

The initial response that latter paved way for eventual administrative re-organisation of states in the region, was in the form of autonomy demanded by the Naga tribal groups in the eastern corner of the region.

Though the subsequent developments in this context are outside the purview of the present analysis, suffice it to say that insurgency in Nagaland speeded up the reorganisation of states. Parts of Naga inhabited areas in south-eastern Arunachal Pradesh, Tuensang area and Naga Hills were merged together and formed the state of Nagaland. This came into effect in 1963. The language bill of Assam became the focus of controversy. This led to the formation of the state of Meghalaya in 1972 (in 1969, the districts of Garo Hills and Untied Khasi and Jaintia Hills became a sub-autonomous unit within Assam state), Lushai Hills from a district became a Union Territory in 1972; Manipur and Tripura from a Union Territory status became full-fledged states in 1972, and the North-Eastern Frontier Agency (prior to 1954, it was known as the North-Eastern frontier tracts) was redesignated as the Arunachal Pradesh and became a Union Territory in 1972.

Thus, the North Eastern India, the name given by British, with the spirit of divide and rule policy in order to accentuate the voluminous contradiction among the people of the region emerged. The same was replicated by India by operating different laws within one state, having tendencies of assertion of national interest and denying reaction of it. In short, the two external forces kept up the people of NE in the frying pan.

NOTES AND REFERENCES

1. Today NE India consists of eight states including Sikkim. Border line and the length (roughly) between: Assam–Bhutan 500 km, Arunachal Pradesh–China 117 km, AP–Burma 525 km, Bangladesh–Assam 200 km, Manipur–Burma 425 km, Mizoram–Bangladesh 275 km, Tripura–Bangladesh 625 km, Meghalaya - Bangladesh 400 km, (Total: 4825 km excluding Sikkim).

2. *East India Human Development Report*, National Council of Applied Economic Research, Oxford University Press, New Delhi, 2004, p.98.
3. *Ibid.*, p.99.
4. *Ibid.*, p.100 & *UNDP* 2000, 01,02,03 and 04, *Human Development Report,* OUP 2000, 012, 02, 03 and 04.
5. *Ibid.*, p.101.
6. *Ibid.*
7. *Ibid.*
8. *Ibid.,* p.102.
9. *Borderlines*, Vol. 1 No. 2, October 2004 p.31.

   Binalakshmi, Editor, opines that the Tripuris are starting arms struggle to flushed out and stop the influx of refugees.
10. *n 4.*
11. *The Seven Sisters of North East India: A Profile*, published on behalf of North East India Coordination Committee for the World Social Forum, 2004 by North Eastern Social Research Centre, 2004, Guwahati.
12. *n* 4.
13. Fourth World means those people whose representatives could not represent to UN as sovereign country.
14. Euthanasia means easy death. So Right to Euthanasia means right to easy death.
15. Internal self-determination is interpreted as a creation of a new state within the nation, External self-determination means sovereignty.

    If the aspirations of the hill people are to be conceptualised on a single scale, the measures would be called 'a quest for identity'. At one end of it is the demand for district autonomy within the existing states like Assam and Manipur. At the other are the movements for independence, which aim at a 'sovereign' countries. What is more important is to note that, although autonomy is a particular form of external relation, its need is felt at a particular stage in the internal development of a community and can never be an independent demand. Precisely because of this, the hill people of Tripura are fighting for a constitutional guarantee for their land and the Kuki are identifying themselves with the statehood demand of Manipur and yet talking of district autonomy. Articulate public opinion in Meghalaya was not satisfied with the autonomous state which indeed separated it from Assam for all practical purposes. The nature of the political aspiration of the hill people would, therefore, have to be assessed in the context of the stages of socioeconomic development of the different groups. What appear to be 'tribal solidarity movements' have a definite socio-economic content.

SK Chaube, *Hill Politics in North East India*, Orient Longman Limited, Patna, 1999, pp.244-245.

16. R. Gopalkrishnan, *The North-East India Land, Economy, and People*, Vikas Publishing House, New Delhi, 1995, p.35.
17. Introduction by Fuller, in Major A. Playfair, *The Garos*, London, 1909, p.XIII.
18. Playfair *op.cit.* pp.10-16.
19. H. Bareh, *The History and Culture of the Khasi People*, Shillong 1967, p.35.
20. Gilchrist McCall, *Anthology Lushai Chrysalist,* London, 1949, p.26.
21. G.A. Grierson, in his report on the *Linguistic Survey of India* (Calcutta, 1904, Vol. III, part III Pp.6-8) insisted on a connection between the Kuki-Chin, the Meitei, the Bodo and the Naga language, all belonging to the Tibeto-Burman family, but was inclined to regard Meitei in the broad category of Kuki-Chin languages.
22. Sachin Roy in his work, *Aspects of Padam-Minyong Culture*, Shillong, 1964, p.259, finds two different cultural strains in the north-western and the rest of the territory.
23. *Ibid.*, p.36.
24. *Ibid.*, p.38.
25. *Ibid.*, p.39
26. *Ibid.* Prof. J.N. Phukan stated that "the communities, who are inhabiting in all parts of NE, majority of them are Tai", in the National Seminar on "Ahom–Shan–Manipuri

Diaspora, – In the 13th century" which was held on 7th & 8th Oct., 1998 at M.U.

27. S.K. Bhuyan, *Anglo-Assames Relations* (1771 to 1826), Gauhati, 1949 p.301.
28. Sanajaoba Naorem, *Manipur Treaties and Documents* (1110-1971) Vol. I, Mittal Publications, New Delhi, 1993 p.17. In the Treaty of Yandaboo, as far as Manipur is concerned it is maintained that "with regard to Manipore, it is stipulated that, should Gumbheer Singh desire to return to that country, he shall be recognized by the king of Ava as Rajah thereof (February 24, 1826)".
29. *Pemberton's Report 1835.*
30. Alexender Mackenzie, Memorandum on the North East Frontier, 1869, cited in his *History of the Relations of the Government with the Hill Tribes of the North-East Frontiers of Bengal,* Calcutta, 1884, p.369.
31. J.M. Scott, *The Tea Story,* London, 1964.
32. Mackenzie, *op.cit*, p.88.
33. Gopalkrishnan, *op.cit.*, p.33.
34. Robert Reid, *History of the Frontier Areas Bordering on Assam from 1883-1941*, Shillong, 1942, p.3 quoting DR Dyall, Commissioner, Chittagong Division.
35. A.S. Reid, *Chin-Lushai Land*, London, 1893, p.1.
36. Mackenzie, *op.cit.,* p.286.
37. Gopalkrishnan, *op.cit.,* Pp.34-35.
38. Dhanabir, L., *Political Participation in Manipur (1940-1984)*, unpublished Ph.D. Thesis submitted to Department of Political Science, Cancchipur: Manipur University, 1994, p.20.

2

POLITICAL ECONOMY OF NORTH-EAST

The people of North-East India, particularly the indigenous people, choose to describe India as an occupying country in the states. They feel that NE state's natural resources except that of some states are being exploited by 'occupant India', and the indigenous population is suffering as a result. It appears to have convinced that Assam's cupful of woes is attributable only to the machination of the 'colonial structure' of the Indian government. Thus, the ULFA argues,

> *"Does India have any answer sheet for solving the burning problems of Assam. Has India done anything to solve the problems like flood, unemployment, deforestation, soil conservation, illegal migration, education and public health in its last fifty years of occupation? Does India honestly admit the value of the looted wanton natural resources from Assam in the good name of development and peace?"*[1]

Again, in a recent newsletter, the ULFA blames the woes of the state on its bureaucrats. The letter states

> *"If we minutely observe all the eco-social erosion of our country since the time of Indian occupation it is realized that these pack of bureaucrats are the masterminds of making Assam a home of sub-*

> *continental illegal economic migrants, think tanks of cunning policy for the looting of wanton natural resources of Assam, playmakers of dividing the society of Assam in the name of the so-called Indian democracy and above all the designers of the blue print of turning Assam to a killing field".*[2]

In the same tune, the Revolutionary People's Front (RPF) also justified the struggle for liberation of Manipur by stating that "The Government of India as it existed in 1947, before the annexation of Manipur to the colonial administration of India. Hence, the Government of India cannot find out a reason whatsoever to level the national liberation movement of Manipur as a separatist movement. The people of Manipur want to honour and disclaimed the exact territory of India as on the 15th August, 1947, that date of its independence, which is in no way includes an inch of the territory of Independence of Manipur".

The organization further stated that national liberation movement of Manipur was seeded since the late 1960s. Thereafter, militant resistance had been physically and openly started by the Meetei State Committee (MSC), which was closely followed by the Revolutionary Government of Manipur (RGM). After the dismantling and disbandment of RGM, the Revolutionary People's Front (RPF is the political wing of the People's Liberation Army of Manipur) was formed on 25 February 1979 and started operating for the liberation of Manipur from the Indian occupation army and Indian colonialism along with several insurgent organizations. In 1978, there had been full scale armed resistance all over the State against the Indian occupation army. It also added that the national liberation movement of Manipur has been consistently opposing the colonial Government of India on political terms and had been struggling against the occupation army of India on military terms since the time of Indian annexation of Manipur in 1949 till to day.[3]

Some states of NE excluding Assam choose to describe them as captive markets of India. All the agricultural products are marginalised due to large scale submerging of agricultural fields on account of constructing Hydro Electric projects. So they become dependent on the agricultural products of areas imported from outside the NE states . For example, Loktak project of Manipur, it was commissioned in 1980 for giving power to outside states. But more than 80,000 acres of agricultural fields were submerged by water. The agricultural products of Loktak areas could give more than Rs.300 crores annually to the state before these fields were submerged.

In Meghalaya, the Khasi Students Union (KSU), the Meghalaya People Human Right Council (MPHRC) and the Heritage Environment Preservation Sites Organisation (HEPSO) now awaits the Uranium Corporation of India Limited (UCIL) to consent to debate on the ill effects of Uranium mining. After throving their own challenge to debate on the issue of the proposed Uranium mining in Domiasial. The KSU President, Mr. Samuel Jyrwa stated that they now want the UCIL to respond and that they will prove their point. Reiterating that Uranium mining will cause health hazards, the three organisations, who maintained their strong opposition to the proposed project have already lined up their own experts to take on the men of UCIL. Till date, the UCIL has not officially complied to the social organisations. Likewise in Manipur and Arunachal Pradesh, people also oppose construction of mega dam. Thus multi national corporations are trying to extract and utilise all the resources of NE states. But today, people no longer remain as silent spectators.

To day all the essential foods are coming from outside the NE region. That means centre has given good amount of money in right hand but it has taken away all what was given from left hand again since they purchase all their essential commodities from the other regiopns of trhe country. So not a single rupee is left in the hands of the people. In short whatever consumed by the people for their day to day needs are from outside states. The same hardship is being faced by the Tripuri and the Naga also.

Problems of North-East India

As far as problems of NE India are concerned, one comes to understand that the political and economic factors are responsible for the problem. Their economy has remained primitive and backward, yet that is not updated. Iinstead, the people of the region are systematically exploited and politically they are suppressed.

Political Problem

The people of the Northeastern region do not consider themselves as equal partners of the Indian Union. They feel that they are being ruled by power that is at the centre like internal colonialism. So there is demand for separation from the Indian Union by the states having sovereign country status before merger and other newly created states demand for special status (Autonomous) within the Indian Union. Their eyes are on Article 370 of the constitution, which is in common parlance known as the Kashmir pattern. Even regional parties have been formed instead of giving loyalties to the national political parties. Each state has not less than two regional political parties. It may be mentioned for Assam that the one-man Tiwari Commission set up to probe Assam disturbances was boycotted by the Assamese public. In its recommendation it said "17.23 Assam should be granted special protection as in Kashmir where no real estate can be acquired by or sold to an outsider". At present there is an act in the state which has replaced the earlier ordinance entitled "The Assam Alienation of Land (Regulation) Ordinance, 1980". Under this act, restriction have been placed through legislation on the acquisition of the immovable property by foreigners in Assam. Considering the peculiarities of Assam, the valley people also deserves the same protection as the tribal belts and blocks in order to protect the interests of the local people. Referring to the Clause 5 of the Article, the Commission said, "Thus restrictions can be imposed not only for the protection of the interests of Scheduled Tribes, but also the interests of the general public".[4]

In the background of the demands raised by different people, as well as, regional parties for the re-evaluation of centre-state relations and granting of more powers to the states, the demand of the states of the North East region for special status cannot be brushed aside by the rulers of the centre in an indifferent way. It must be admitted that notwithstanding a number of provisions in the constitution for safeguarding the identity of small ethnic groups, the people of this region have the apprehension of losing their identity. The stoic indifference of the centre to the legitimate aspirations of the people has created this feeling. The six-year old Assam agitation on the foreigner's issue is a pointer to this apprehension. The same movement has been done in Manipur by All-Manipur Students Union (AMSU) though it lasted only a short while. Measures can be taken to remove this apprehension provided there is political will to do so, which is lacking so much.

There is also a feeling that even the constitution has been discriminatory against the small states, as they have no equal representation in the Council of States. To remove these apprehensions one can suggest that India should be declared a multi-national state. The very name Council of States, in a way implies that all states-big or small should have equal representation. At present, the North East states have very small representation. It is mostly filled up with representatives of major states, which makes the voice of the states of this region so feeble. Indian constitution is unitary one, but has a federal look. It must be made really federal.[5]

Though Prafulla Mishra gives his views in favour of federal structure to resolve the ongoing situation of armed conflict in the North East[6], Prof. N. Sanajaoba, eminent scholar of NE subscribes his views that the political issue of the North East has been misconceived as 'law and order' or, at most 'internal security' issue, whereas it bears the intrinsic essence of de-colonisation and national liberation war euphemistically, known as secessionism. The issue is very deep and the fault lines are profound. The sustenance of the issue for more than four decades itself indicates that human rights violations and the twisted perceptions are merely symptoms of the malaise.

The available evidence, the demand structure, the historical facts and the pattern of union governments' response to the issue make it amply clear that the decades-old political violence, as espoused by the liberation army, has been a consequence of unresolved political questions.

Historical evidence very clearly stipulates that (i) Manipur and Tripura had been annexed to the Indian political fold, after two years of Indian independence; (ii) Assam became a part of British India not by her choice but by the choice of Burma and British, who signed the Treaty of Yandaboo in 1826; (iii) the ethnic tribes who remained in the excluded hill areas of Assam fused themselves in the last five decades into nationhood and claimed independence prior to the passage of Indian Independence Act of 1947; and (iv) British-created India has been a totally different entity from the original Indian nation that continued for centuries in the Gangetic basin. The British-created India has been a deliberate political creation, unlike the homogenous Indian nation, based on Aryabrata. The issue is, therefore, not secession, but about fixing the region to India by hammer and tongs.[7]

In short, major insurgency groups in NE India is associated with political discourse of decolonisation. B.S. Butola aptly remarked that the emergence of regional political parties and a large number of insurgent movements too indicate the underlying resentment of the people against such approaches of development, (triple objectives of India – economic development, defence of India's sovereignty and national integration). Further he states

> *"It is, therefore, imperative to understand the feeling of the people of the region with human consideration and it will be fallacious to call the troubles in the region as a mere law and order problem or the handiwork of the foreign and Indian forces".*[8]

State Terrorism through Black Laws

A consequence of the inefficiency of political discourse is terrorism, Government vilified the movement grew out of locally based groups giving voice to various grivances, mainly to those scessionist – though they are in the categories of belegrents. To counter them, Government also terrories the people and has done many inhuman actions against their own people. So, terrorising of the people of North East by the Government is done in an organised systematic way. The display of sophisticated weapons with columns of Army marching in full public view with armoured vehicles, manned by the officers and soldiers speaking foreign languages (Hindi & English, not known to the common people) instills fear in the mind of the general public. The Armed Forces are given sweeping powers by the Armed Forces Special Power's Act (AFSPA), 1958 which has been extended to all states of the North East India after amendment in 1972. The AFSPA is the reincarnation of the British colonial Law, the Armed Forced (Special Power) Ordinance, 1942 which was promulgated on the wake of the Japanese aggression in World War II under which a responsible military officer not below the rank of a 'captain' can cause death or extra judicial murder. Under section 4 of AFSPA, even a Havildar is empowered to commit extra judicial murders and arrest has been granted under Section 6 of this Act after most of the areas in North East are declared as disturbed areas. In addition to the deployment of the heavily armed state police and state rifles, army and paramilitary forces are also deployed in North-East region.[9] The army paramilitary forces and police take every opportunity to terrorise the general masses by way of combing operation, raping and killing women, wanton arrest, illegal detention, killing while in police custody, killing of innocents in indiscriminate firing, etc. Many innocent people have lost their lives in indiscriminate firing. People also bear the brunt of the torture by the armed forces and paramilitary forces.[10]

Economic Problem

It is well known that the NE region has abundance of resources. Yet, the region displays the characteristics of growth stagnancy, both in absolute and relative terms.

There are a number of factors associated with this phenomena. These can be identified as

i. geographical inertia; unfavorable location factors from the point of view of markets, accessibility, investment, development and so on;

ii. inadequate transportation and communication infrastructure and facilities;

iii. scale and extent of natural calamities such as recurring annual floods affected the entire region, thereby accentuating dependency;

iv. large-scale immigration in the region establishing political, economic and social framework, particularly in the states of Assam, Tripura and to an extent in the state of Meghalaya;

v. multi-ethnic, multi-linguistic and multi-religious composition of the population of the region added significantly towards the complexities in the developmental process; and

vi. political aspirations of the various population groups and sub-groups have frequently created ethnic clash in the region.

The Northeast states predominantly rural in character, the region's agricultural scenario is dominated by mono-cropping that occupied approximately 85 percent of the total cultivated area of the region. Farming techniques are either outdated or too traditional (like Jhum cultivation) to have any decisive impact on productivity and production. Only 37.2 percent of the area was cultivated with Assam occupying the major part of it. Of this, only 17.6 percent is under the High Yielding programmes that use approximately 3.5 kg. of fertilizers (very low as compared to the national average on the use of fertilizers).

The agricultural landscape of the region, particularly in the hill sections was dominated by Jhum cultivation and consequently have acute soil erosion and conservation problems. Jhum or shifting cultivation was very much a part of the life and culture of the population of the hill sections of the region and as such was very difficult to replace. Spread of education and other socio-economic welfare programmers can slowly overcome the problem. But that is not in a satisfactory level.[11]

Limited availability of cultivable land and the level of technology (low) as well as the scale of inputs have remained the major constraints of agricultural development in the region. Besides, population growth – higher than the rest of the country – has remained constantly high. This retarded the limited effort. As a result, the area that was once a food-surplus zone, has now become a chronic food deficit area.

The growth and development problems in the region are of a different footing altogether from the rest of the country. As long as the administrative units remained either as a part of the pre 1963 composite state of Assam or as a union territory, there were not significant financial constraints. However, with the attainment of statehood, many of the states in the region, in order to meet the rising aspirations of the population and requirements for development were unable to mobilise the additional resources. The existing resources could not be developed for want of adequate transport infrastructure or as such devoted substantial part of their annual budgetary outlays on strengthening the communication linkages in the respective states. It was complicated by the fact that the income-multiplier process was negligible if not totally absent in the region. Known existing resources though abundant, provided very few alternatives. As a result, there was insignificant participation in the manufacturing sector of the economy.

Apart from the oil refineries and tea, the region had a number of on-going large and medium scale projects in various stages of completion. The operational ones include, a jute mill in Tripura, modernisation of tea industry in the secondary belts of Tripura, in Cachar along with introduction of tea in Nagaland and Meghalaya at an experimental scale, introduction of coffee and rubber in Mizoram and Meghalaya, cotton spinning mills in Manipur, ginger processing plants in Mizoram and so on. Of the ongoing schemes, the most important ones are the cement projects in the Garo Hills and Jaintia Hills in Meghalaya, glass factory in Nagaland, fruit processing and canning in Arunachal Pradesh and so on.

On the whole, the factors that inhibited the development effort in the region can be identified as –

Elements of isolation as reflected in the region's geography, society and politics; area-hills and plain sections; population-tribals and non-tribals as well as the problems centred around locals and outsiders; socio-economic resistances as well as structural and institutional rigidities in the region's society; a very high percentage of the population live in the rural areas and are directly dependent upon agriculture;

Infrastructual deficiencies, market imperfections and administrative drawbacks, repressions of local, national and international forces on the region's activities;

Role and function of the political processes in participation, representation and decision-making and insignificant role of the region's urban centers in generating opinions and ideas to foster and encourage economic growth and industrialisation.[12]

A View on Indian Political System and Economic Planning

India was artificially formed as a union of varied political units without the essential elements of nation and nationalism. It has no common religion, culture, language and political aspiration, though maximum effort is being made in the nation building process. So the question of narrow nationalism, chauvinism, ethnic and cultural prejudice arose in the minds of the new generation with economic crisis, crisis of ideology of progress and malcontent morality. It is irrational to expect that our people have had such perception among them who are Indian by birth.

India, like other liberal democracies of the West such as Great Britain, the United States, France, Germany and Sweden, has liberal democratic system with the characteristics of more than one political party, election at fixed intervals, not subject to tight governmental control over pressure groups, trade unions and other voluntary associations, civil liberties and independence of judiciary. As a result, the mass media, i.e. radio, television, and newspapers enjoy a considerable amount of independence. But it will be argued that the continuance of such administration in which the party and its leaders are standing behind the constitution, will convert the system into a totalitarian one. That is why the country was being ruled for a long time by only one party based on the single party principle. Moreover, economy is centrally directed. Civil liberties are sharply curtailed, even mass media is strictly controlled by the government as well as voluntary associations are subject to close governmental control. It is not the same to all the states of India. Some are enjoying modern democracy and some are under the totalitarian administrative system.

Due to the failure of identifying the existing system, people demanded visible polity in which the real norms and political formula, which are accepted by all the political actors of world, should be followed and applied. What is going on in the plan period? India borrowed plan framework from the then Soviet Russia model which did not suit Indian conditions and too much reliance on planners did not go hand in hand with a society having considerable size of private sector activity. There is a lack of clarity in the minds of many ruling elites that India is composed of many states, very far from them, they completely forget that they are ministers for those states also. They neglected human resources, the need for technological change and proper measure to contain population for particular places which do not belong to them. It breeds the tendency of sub-nationalism and nation. The result is that maximum people of India have been stating about regional imbalance. As a consequence,the region is witnessing the movement for regional autonomy and secession.

Basically, the people who got maximum values will always give positive response. On the contrary, the people who are not in value based political system automatically will be completely indifferent from the system. This formula is perception not illusion. So even a child supposed to follow this path should also be ready to challenge it. But majority of the intellectuals from North East India try to justify the political system, even though they were in agony and graveyard. How long will they regret and keep their trust to the union government with verbal promises which were never translated into action. Why did they keep their mouths shut even when the Indian Prime Minister had publicly admitted that the Central Government had been meeting out step motherly treatment to the north-eastern region of the country since 1950. Other ministers and leaders of the centre had on a number of occasions observed that the pace of development in the North East had been tardy. There had been lip sympathy galore for central leaders, but hardly there is any worthwhile concrete implementation. That is why showing the full picture of India's development and its syndrome of negligence to North East India of fundamental importance is quite necessary for better understanding.

When one comes to North East India from other states, they can easily come to understand that North-East is in a standstill not moving at all. Here one can have many unhappy tales of human sufferings, political instability, economic disruptions, social tensions and communal misdeeds. These are the handiworks of the central political leaders. Instances of such step-motherly treatment and apathy towards the entire north-eastern region are a legion, but whenever each states of the region raises demands for self-assertion they are dubbed as parochial. In 1997, Deve Gowda, the then Prime Minister of India could feel the pulse of the people of this region, that prompted him to offer Rs.6,100 crore economic package to the region. The Prime Minister of India, when he visited Manipur on 20th November 2004, he sanctioned Rs.2777.68 crores to Manipur for development projects. But the question that arises is "Can the ruling elites suppress the increasing sense of alienation from the mainstream of India and how long could India give economic booster to this region while its economic condition is gloomy ?". No one in the region could expect a better future for them if he or she analysed the economic diary of India since 1950.

Everybody has witnessed the era of economic planning with nine full five-year plans while the tenth plan is going to complete its last year in 2007. The first five-year plan was launched on April 1, 1951. The highest priority was given to such infrastructures as transport and communication, energy generation, irrigation facilities, education, health and medical facilities, social security measures etc. In the second plan, a high priority was accorded to basic and capital goods industries. As a result, industrial machinery and machine tools, electrical engineering, transport equipments and iron and steel industries were developed in the public sector on a considerable scale. These industries involve massive investment which would not have come from private sector. The general index of industrial production (bases 1980-81 = 100) went up from

0.48 in 1960-61 to 252 in 1994-95, the largest having been recorded by chemical industry.

Another significant achievement of planning has been the contribution to agrarian reforms and results of green revolution. Since 1966, the main emphasis had been laid on introduction of new technology in agricultural productivity. The use of irrigation, fertilizers, pesticides, high yielding seeds, cheap credit supply, use of various subsidized implements of farm mechanization, etc. on the one hand and increasing rates of procurement value of produce under price support have come into existence. Programme of government, in fact, revolutionized agriculture and turned the country's status into a self sufficient food economy from the one that used to hunt for import of food grains from PL 480 funds of USA and other foreign sources to feed the hungry millions of the country until late sixties of the current century.

However, all were not well with the economy and the achievement of 54 years of planning has been subjected to serious limitations mainly on account of defective policy frames, implementation failures and misuse of public funds. Our planners and ruling elites could not treat evenly all the states. They were always at stake for their concerned states, it led to uneven development among the states of the country. That is why the question of regional imbalance arose. The planners completely neglected human resources and proper measure to contain population and the need of technology changes. The planned process relied too much on licenes, quotas and restrictions that give way to rampant corruption, inefficiency and misuse of tax-payers' money. An unholy alliance between the politician, the contractor and the bureaucrat set in.[13]

Moreover, many cases of corruption committed by ruling elites on one hand and deficit finance on the other are weighing the two sides of the scale. It is very unfortunate for all the people of India in general, and those in the North-East India in particular. The corruption relating to unaccounted deals has been rampant in the country. Thus, the Harshad Mahta security scam of around Rs.400 crore, Rs.64 crore Jain Hawala scam, Rs.23 crore JMM bribery case, $ 21 million St. Kitts forgery case, $1 lakh Lakhubai cheating case, Rs.3.66 crore Sukh Ram cash recovery scam, Rs.133 crore Urea import scam, Rs.100 crore Bihar Fodder scam, Rs.200 crore Assam LOC scam and other cases of telecommunication scam, television subsidy scam, etc. are also the infamous events recorded in the economic diary of half a century.

The deficit financing came to be looked upon as an important source of financing the plans. From just Rs.333 crore in the first plan, deficit rose to Rs.3360 crore in the fifth plan and to Rs.34,132 crore in the seventh plan. In the international trade front, the balance of payments situation which was much comfortable in the first plan with a deficit of Rs.42.3 crore started assuming serious dimension to Rs.3010 crore at the end of Fifth Plan and to Rs.12,764 crore in the year 1992-93. The external debt position started getting from bad to worse and aggregated a staggering amount of Rs.3,10,319 crore in 1995-96.

Though the deficit financing is curving down and making up in time, one cannot deny the fact that some fruits have been reaped from economic reforms by a few states during the last decades. That is not based on greatest happiness of greatest number. All the seven states of North East India are remaining far behind in comparison with others. Here one can make argument that the country's foreign exchange reserves which came down to just $ 2 billion in 1991 have now reached around $ 19 billion in 1996. The national income grew by more than 5 per cent in 1992-93 and has increased by 6.2 per cent in 1995-96 as against a near stagnation in the earlier years; the inflationary rate which reached the peak of 17 per cent in 1991-92 came down to 7.6 per cent in January, 1997 and the fiscal deficit which was 8.5 per cent of SDP in 1990-91 has come down to 6 per cent in 1995-96. But the answer is that other Indians from advanced states are many times as well-off as an average people of North-East in terms of income terms. That is why, Sri H.D. Deve Gowda, the then Prime Minister of India,while laying the foundation stone of the fourth bridge over the Brahmaputra at Kulajan near Dhamaji in Lakhimpur district on Wednesday, (22-1-1997), did not hesitate to say that neglect of the earlier Governments at the centre towards the need of the North East has kept the region backward compared to other regions of the country and assured the mammoth crowd that this apathetic attitude would not be allowed to continue.[14] Kaushik Basu, Professor of Economics at Cornell University, recently remarked rightly that it was the fruit of both political and economic system based on unsocialism. In his experience, India's policies were born out of an uneasy compromise between Gandhi's dreams of a simple, village-based economy and Nehru's Fabian ideals of the welfare state with a heavy-industry foundation, based on what he had learnt at Harrow and Cambridge. Nehru, would have found his effort on a bureaucratic structure that was a leftover of the Raj. Years later, Nehru would tell Galbraith that he was the last Englishman to rule India. In short, a large planning effort was started and handed over to a bureaucracy, which was large and ever expanding. Moreover the welfare state was never adopted and 'socialism' became a word that had to be used repeatedly to make up for this lacunae.

Taking into account the period of the Vajpayee government since 1998 Lok Sabha election, the BJP rule has lasted for six years. This six-year rule has pursued a combination of communal politics, pro-rich economic policies and craven support to US imperialism. They are not in the lower position of corruption in comparison with the past. The Vajpayee government has set new records in high level corruption. The Tehelka tape exposure revealed shockingly how kickbacks in defence deals are a regular occurrence. For the first time the President of a ruling party was seen receiving a bribe on camera. Instead of cleaning up the system, the government launched a vindictive campaign to harass Tehelka.[15]

One of the biggest scandals involving thousands of crores of rupees has been the way the US-64 schemes of the UTI was allowed to collapse, depriving millions of small investors of their hard earned savings.

The Vajpayee government is known as a government of privatization schemes. Every public sector sale and the disinvestments of shares are wrapped in dubious methods, shady deals and under-valuation of assets. The VSNL, the Baloco and Centaur Hotel sales are some examples. The CAG report on the Centaur Hotel sale has exposed the racketeering which has cost the government exchequer heavily.

Corruption has hit all sectors affected by privatization: telecom, cit, sugar and so on. The massive stamp paper swindle involved the sale of machinery from the government security press at Nasik to Telgi.[16]

No item is beyond the greed of the BJP-RSS combined. A majority of the 3,850 petrol pumps and gas agencies allotted through the ministry of petroleum were found to benefit BJP-RSS functionaries and their relatives.

Another stint of BJP-RSS rule in the name of the NDA would mean facilitating the advance of a Handutva-based authoritarianism which spelled danger for secularism, democracy and social justice. It would mean more reactionary economic policies which will threaten the livelihood of millions. The BJP rule would mean bringing in imperialism and foreign capital in a big way into our economy and society, further eroding national sovereignty and thwarting any semblance of an independent foreign policy.

After BJP, Congress policies could not give alternative to the masses. The Congress Party ruled the country for over four decades. Its policies and record of government contributed to the present plight of the people and the country. Its failure to strengthen the foundations of democracy, secularism, federalism and its anti-people policies laid the basis for the rise of the BJP and its coalition government. The Congress has not learnt lessons from the past. The Congress advocates economic policies which are not different from the BJP. The Congress-run state governments such as the UPF government in Kerala are pursuing policies which promote privatization and liberalization. The people opposed to the oppressive BJP rule expect a firm defence of secularism and democratic values, not a vacillating and compromising role. They will rally to policies which provide them with a state in economic development and which is an alternative to the BJP's right wing, pro-big business policies.[17]

Anti-National Economic Policies

At no time in independent India so much has been done for the rich and so little for the poor. The policies of the all governments have led to the systematic transfer of resources and assets from the people to a narrow circle of big business, big traders, speculators and foreign companies.[18]

The sale of public sector assets has meant a transfer of public resources to private hands.

The fiscal and taxation policies have led to enormous concessions for the rich and cut backs for the ordinary people. While a bonanza has been provided for the affluent, savings of the middle class, the pensioners and ordinary citizens have dwindled due to the cut in interest rates of bank deposits and provident and pension funds.

Rural India is in distress because of the acute agrarian crisis. Recent estimates shows that the total loss to farmers due to crash in prices is Rs.1,16,000 crores annually. The per capita availability of food grains per annum as come down from 184.5 kg. in 1997 to 152.1 kg. in 2001 – almost the same level of consumption that existed at the time of the Bengal famine in 1943.

The Vajpayee government has assiduously worked to dismantle the public sector. The most profitable PSUs like VSNL, Balco, etc. are being sold off cheaply to Indian and foreign monopolies. The privatization drive has affected all sectors telecom, cit., transport, power and even public services.

In every budget presented by the Vajpayee government since 1999, the rich have been given direct tax concessions. The top 100 big business houses saved taxes to the extent of Rs.6853.64 crores in a single year 2000-01. Excise and customs duties have been reduced on air-conditioners, refrigerators, gold, silver, diamonds and automobiles. On the other hand, an additional duty of Re.1 per litre of diesel, a steep increase in postal rates, matches, textiles and administered price increase of LPG and Kerosene and fertilizers were announced, imposing a heavy burden on the common people. The bonanza of pre-election snops have also benefited the affluent.[19]

The abolition of quantitative restrictions on imports and steep cuts in customs and import duties have badly affected agriculture and made small and medium industries vulnerable to the global market and spelt ruin for these sectors.

Vicious Attacks on Peoples

If there is one single episode which reveals the callousness towards the poor and the inhuman character of the BJP-led government's policies, it is the dismantling of the public distribution system. The curtailment at the PDS was cruel and deprived millions of the urban and rural poor of cheap and essential foodstuff. This government, which promised to eliminate hunger, has presided over large-scale hunger affecting millions of people.

The government hoarded six crore tonnes of foodgrains in 2002 rather than distribute it to the hungry rural poor who were badly hit by the draught in recent years. Instead, the prices of rice and wheat in all categories for the BPL and APL were hiked up periodically. The same government thought it fit to export one crore tones of foodgrains at below poverty line prices rather than distribute it to the needy people. Subsidized export of foodgrains for foreigners and keeping the poor hungry – this is the new version of independence of the BJP.

The successor government surrendered to the rich countries and subsequent implementation of the WTO regulations has been disastrous for the Indian agriculture and the farmers. The abolition of quantitative restrictions and the drastic lowering of import duties have led to price fluctuation for many agricultural commodities. Suicides by farmers have been rampant all around the country.

Scourge of Unemployment

The government's economic policies have made unemployment the biggest problem for the people. Rural unemployment, unemployment for the youth, educated unemployment, unemployment for women and loss of existing jobs in the public sector and the organized sector have blighted the lives of millions of people. The rate of growth of employment has been a dismal 1.13 per cent and BJP rule. Of the 41 million registered job seekers in the employment exchange in 2000-01, only 99,000 got jobs. Existing employment is being done away with. There was a decline of 8.34 lakh jobs in the organized sector between 1998 and March 2002. According to the Planning Commission, an estimated 16 per cent of the youth will be unemployed at the end of the Tenth Plan. In rural areas agricultural workers and women are faced with sharply reduced workdays per year.

Whatever stated in the above pages is the tragedy of the nation as a whole; here one could imagine what would happen in the North East states, and that they are completely neglected by the centre. They are politically oppressed and economically exploited. Even people are in the real process of internal colonialism of India. It has been witnessed from the beginning of historical time in all hierarchical and class societies that every economic policies have aimed either at consolidating existing structures of dominance or at forging with the perceived requirements of the ruling classes. In fact, economy is never independent of class interest. It is a well known fact that in pre-colonial North East the people were subject to exploitation by feudal rulers who enjoyed unlimited powers. The dominating form of economy was subsistence economy. The production for them were in a state of stagnation and were unable to promote any technical progress. When British colonialists arrived, the exploitation was stepped up. The decaying traditional economical methods were not replaced there by more progressive forms which could help the people of NE overcome its backwardness and stagnation. There were practically no industries that could ensure independent development and help to overcome backwardness.

In this present-day North East still carry on the burden of its colonial past. It has been passing through various abnormalities and crisis. The present all round crisis is probably due to the outcomes of the very strategy followed by the Indian ruling class and their collaborators during the Past 58 years. The neo-liberal economic reforms adopted by the Indian ruling class as a part of the imperialist driven globalisation have further worsened the condition of the people in multiple ways.

Backward and deprived North East is trapped in a vicious circle.

Transportation and Communication

Transportation and Communication is inadequate both at the inter-regional level and with the rest of the country. It has often been referred to as one of the important factors that retarded the economic development or the region. This inadequacy along with the distribution pattern of the terrain features has been responsible to a large extent for the neglect of the rail-road development in the region. Major General Samay Ram (Retd.) rightly stated that "due to the mountaneous terrain covered with thick jungles, these region is inaccessible. No efforts were made by the centre even after independence to develop rail and road communications to connect them to the mainland. The people of this region therefore were isolated and neglected. Prolonged neglect and isolation led to a sense of alienation, a fertile situation for the onset of insurgency."

In other words, the pressure or adequate infrastructural facilities has become an important prerequisite for sustained economic development of the region It has become all the more important for the North Eastern region where industrial activity based on locally available resources formed an important income generating alternative. A better infrastructural network would reduce the impact of isolation and inaccessibility while it will encourage investments in the region – both within and from outside. However, as is obvious from the politico-administrative patterns, commercial exploitation of resources, movements of population and developments in general in the region, certain district traces of bias have been forcefully implanted, so that, there continued (from 1826 onwards) sub-regional variations and disparities that persistently influenced the developmental policy formulations and their implementation. The impact was in the form of socio-economic instability with weak and tenuous communication links.

Industries in North East Region

The region as of today continues to have a weak industrial base (Mizoram and Arunachal Pradesh have only cottage and handicraft industries). Despite the State's effort, regional imbalances dominate the region's industrial scenario. The available incentives have proved to be inadequate on-the face of locational disadvantages and communication shortcomings. Moreover, shortage of raw material and the needed market attractions are quite absent in the region.

Till 1987, bulks of region's industrial activities were in the form of small scale and cottage industries. Large scale and medium scale industries continued to be located in the state of Assam. Other states, under the influence of the factors of location and transport linkages, were able to concentrate only on the small scale and cottage handloom industries. Most of the industries, barring tea and traditional cottage industries, were of recent (post independence) origin and their impact on the regional economics was significant. These industries can be summed up as –

Tea located in Assam and Tripura;

Petro-chemical complexes and refineries located in Assam;

Jute mills in Assam and Tripura;

Sugar mills in Assam and Manipur, (Sugar mill of Manipur has closed down since last decade);

Cement plants in Assam and Meghalaya;

Paper and pulp plants in Assam, Nagalanad and Mizoram;

Coal fields in Assam and Meghalaya; and

Fertiliser plant in Assam.

Moreover, taking one from the factory sector (that is those units employing 20 persons without power and 20 persons with power) the region's share in the national total comes only to about 2.12 per cent of which Assam has about 82 per cent, Tripura about 12.5 per cent and all other states combined have about 5.5percent. It indicates that industrial sector, the main pivot of economic development of NE region is really far behind in comparison with other states of India. So the people of NE India are economically backward and maximum numbers of people are based on Agriculture.

Potential Small-Scale Industries

The region has immense potential for developing agro-based and forest product-based industries but they are useless because of not providing subsidiary assistance and unutilisation of the locally available raw materials. Apart from tea, jute, and sugarcane, the region has important cash crops like turmeric, ginger, chillies, areca not, and cashew nuts and so on, that can be used as raw materials for quite a number of food processing units in the small scale sector. Moreover, with nearly 47 per cent of the area under forest, there existed a wide range of forest products on which many ancillary units can be started. In addition to it, the region has favourable agro-climatic conditions that are conducive to large-scale horticultural operations. These climatic elements, in the hill sections of the region, offer a year-round production of fruits and vegetables. These can form the basis of profitable food processing units. But these are the dreams of the people which could not yet be put into reality.

From these political and economic problems which are being faced by the people of NE India, their anger and frustration have been compounded day by day. In addition to the the backwardness in agriculture and low industrial development, the provisions for infrastructure are also inadequate, and people don't foresee any prospect in the coming future. So they conceive the idea that the Government of India has given step-motherly treatment to them. It may also be one of the most important root causes of insurgency in NE India.

Migration

The concept of "Migration" is actually the net-product of two dimensionally opposite ideas, viz. "Immigration" and "Emigration". The people who are inflowed during a particular period to the place of enumeration it termed as "immigrants", whereas those who outflowed from the place of enumeration is termed as "emigrants". Here we shall confine ourselves mainly within the immigratory movement. So, the migration of the North Eastern region of India is concerned with the immigratory movements in the region. From the census data we have observed that the share of migrants to the total population of the North Eastern region of India varies throughout the period 1901-1991. The proportion has steadily increased from around 17 per cent in 1901 to slightly more than 23 per cent in 1931. But from 1951 onwards it is declining. It was 15.62 per cent in 1951 and 5.36 per cent in 1991. The population of the region is recorded as 33.50 million in 2001 census. So we may expect the region would have got around 16 lakh migrants, if not more according to the 2001 census.[20]

As far as migration in NE India is concerned, the problem faced by the region is only the problem of foreign migrants and migrants from other states of India not the intra-regional migrants.

Migration and forced assimilation is also the root of insurgency in North East India because they create demographic imbalance. The sons of the soil have their legitimate fears that if the influx continues, they will soon become minority in their own state. It is happening to Assam and Tripura mainly. But for Tripura, assimilation is over. In other words, Tripura is not for the Tripurees, it is for Bengalis only. Large-scale immigration from Bangladesh remains a serious problem in Assam. According to a recent study, a total of 1,298,754 illegal foreign migrants have entered into Assam only between 1951 and 1991. The rate of population growth in the region has remained continuously high. This is evident from the fact that the region at the dawn of the present century had only 4.1 million. This increased to 26 million in 1981. Population growth between 1901 and 1951 remained more or less static at 2 per cent annual growth, but between 1951 and 1981 it accelerated, so that a population which took four decades to double, trebled in the following three decades. This acceleration in population growth in the region has been due to heavy influx of immigrants as in the states of Assam, Tripura and Meghalaya.[21]

Some Indicators of Underdevelopment in NEI

Basically dependency theories have offered several arguments to explain why the development of the advanced capitalists countries produces underdevelopment in the Third World. It means that certain countries self-sustaining growth, or expansion, but can only those countries that dominate them (the advanced countries). That is why the third world countries are not underdeveloped, but underdeveloped. The same argument lies within the nation also i.e. inter-state disparities within the Nation. Within the theory of dependency, there are major tenets. They are surplus extraction, unequal exchange, dependent capitalist development, the centre-periphery model etc. etc.

One of the most striking facts about the various indicators of welfare in the NEI region is trailing behind in almost all the indicators from the rest of the country. Notwithstanding, relatively rapid economic growth in India and more so in the post reform period, the pace of growth in NE part of India has been almost stagnant and even slowing down with respect to certain sectors of the regional economy. Some indicators are discussed below:

Slow Growth of State Domestic Product

One of the prominant features of the NEI economy is the slow growth in the state domestic product and over the years the gap is gradually 'increasing'. Per capita income generation and over the years the gap between the region and the national average is increasing. For example in 1950-51, the per capita income in Assam was 4 percent above the national average. In 1998-99, it was 41 percent below the national average at 1980-81 prices, between 1980 and 1990, per capita income at 1980 prices grew by 20 percent in Assam compared with 40 percent for all India. Bewteen 1980 and 1998, per capita income in Assam grew by 10 percent compared with 39 percent for all India (Assam Development Report, 2002).

A cursory look at the data of NSDP(Net State Domestic Product) has been gradually declined over the years. Gradual decline of NSDP in the 1990's show the nature of dependent accumulation in NE region. It shows that the rate of accumulation in NE has slowed down and reached far below the national average in case of most of the states of NE. This shows that the state with its leadership in transforming economy in capitalistic modes of production has not fully been able to gear itself up as a manager of surplus. This further means (i) state is not able to enlarge economic surplus(in rural, urban or overall) (ii) transfer it among sectors(iii) to be extracted so as to compel increases in either size or the proportion of it i.e. inter-sectoral transfers. The decline in NSDP cripples the state from becoming repository of development and potential of productive forces.[22]

Low Per Capita Income

Per capita income, which has been accepted as yardstick of standard of living of the people, in comparision to the national income of NE there is a large gap between the regions income and the national income. Against the all India PCI of Rs. 14,712 in 1998-99, as given in the *Economic Survey* for 2000-2001, Assam's figure was Rs 8,700, Tripura's was Rs 9,187, Manipuris was Rs. 10,599, Arunachal's was Rs 12,929 and Meghalaya's was Rs 10,607, Mizoram's figure for 1997-98 was Rs 11,667. No official figures for Nagaland, were available. These figures indicate that all states of the NE region are placed below the national average in per capita income. From these data one can infer that for the various classes of the population. This decline also shows underdevelopment of productive forces within the mode of production. This further points out that the productive forces are on an external support system.[23]

High Dependence on Agriculture

The economy of the NEI heavily depends upon the agriculture sector. More than 70 per cent of the population of the region depends upon on agriculture for its livelihood, cultivators and agriculture labourers account for 73.8 per cent in Arunachal Pradesh, 65.8 per cent in Assam, 68.7 per cent in Manipur, 73.3 per cent in Nagaland as against 68.5 per cent in all India average as per 1981 census. The proportion of NEI states is relatively higher than other states of India.

High dependence on agriculture in NEI demostrates that domestic and peripheral modes of production continues to engage in the larger number of workforces in rural, semi-urban and intermediary transactions of food supply economics. Such economics based on share cropping and community - holding lands points to an increased pressure on land. The produce of such a mode of production is more or less restricted to producing food for cash cropping peasants and pauperized rural labours. Local food and surpluses are exported and hence it does not generate money income. Absence of industrialisation in an appropriate form has further magnified the dependence on the demostic modes of production for the larger section of the populace. The scenario of the peasants in the distress political economy of subsistence is compounded by an absence of industry. In short, one could see only in the states of NE having urbanisation without industralisation.

High Dependence on Centre and Low Revenue Generation

The North-Eastern states enjoy some special privileges in the matter of grants and loans from the centre. The low revenue generated from its own sources in its total revenue receipts coupled with the special status enjoyed by the states has led to the over dependence of the states on the centre. For example, in the case of Assam, a total revenue generated by the state government is declining from about 40 per cent at the beginning of the 90s decade to just 30 per cent at the end of it. This is the result of a lower annual growth rate of 12.5 per cent in states own revenue receipts than that of central revenue transfers 16.4 per cent (Assam Development Report 2002). In addition, the composition of central transfers show a decline in the share of state plan transfers and share taxes; to be covered up mainly by centrally sponsored schemes and non-plan grants.

The fact of low revenue generation shows that the formal structure of the state cannot appear in increasing portion of the resources collected, by whatever agencies, at the source from the tax payer. The involution of the state and the sphere of public finance can not ensure that for every unit increase in the informal structures, i.e. business, houses, farm and producers etc. on whom state has little control, the formal state structure does not have a commensuate increase. It produces the gap between revenues collected by the state and other non-state and informal and socio-economic units. In other words, state in the context of NEI cannot develop a formal apparatus of financial responsibility for various section of income generating populace and therefore remains dependent on the centre.

Poverty and Negative Growth of Market

The states in NE are characteriased by high incidence of poverty, specially rural poverty. The Planning Commission expert group headed by Prof. Lakdawala made an estimation of poverty in the region. As per the group 36.5 per cent of the total population of the region is below povety line (BPL) and the population was only 0.38 per cent higher than the national average.

High incidents of poverty shows that the proportion which benefits from process of development is very less because the occupational structure remains dependent upon investment from outside. The low yield of productive resources from occupations segmented social structure and favours only a few and those few have nexus with the market. One can term the situation as a negative growth of market and employment that is the result of the dependent mode of production.

Poor Status of Basic Services

The NE region is also characterised by the deteriorating living conditions. Health and education related services are low if one compares with the developed states of India like Kerala. unavailability of basic services has affected the quality of life in the region. The best example is the Assam which ranks 12 among 16 states where ordered in descending order of Human Development Index (HDI) and Gender Development Index (GDI). Rural and Rurban disparity is very high on several of the indicators. Like expectancy at birth is 54.1 in rural as compared to 63.3 in urban areas, 52 per cent of the children are underweight in rural compared to 37 per cent in urban areas.[24]

Major Problems of the Manipuris outside Manipur: Bishnupriya Issues

Origin of the conflict

It is an undisputed fact that Bishnupriya commonly known as Kalashaya, came to Manipur during the reign of King Pamheiba and started to settle at Lamangdong. They came to Manipur during the different reigns of the Kings. Many of the princes of Manipur had good relationship with them. They even took shelter in Cachar and Bangladesh during the time of seven years devastation (A.D. 1819-1826)

It is also well known that the Meitrabak was renamed as Manipur in 17th Century (1716 Fairengi 13ni Panba, Pakhangba Laihui) when Shantidas came to the land.[20] And all the inhabitants were commonly known as Manipuris. The maximum number of Kalashaya population fled away during the seven years devastation in order to save their lives. The Meetei followed their suits. That is why both the communities were settling in different parts of Assam, Trípura and Bangladesh after Auwa Lal (the Burmese War). They were living together with full understanding, love and affection. But the conflict in between the two communities aroused in the recent time of the history of Manipur. The reason is why. The conflict is deeply rooted after suffixing and affixing the word Manipuris to Bishnupriya. It seems to pollute the identity of the Manipuris. That means, creation of identity crisis to the Manipuris and as such compelled to overcome it.

How Kalashaya became Bishnupriya? The Question of Conflict did not arise in Manipur Why?

During the period of King Bheigyachandra, Lamangdong was renamed as Bishnupur because of constructing the Bishnu Temple there. A good number of Kalashaya were enrolled as devotees of Vaishnavism. So they were called as Bishnupriya. The full details of it could be found from the chronicles or puya known as "Kalisharon", which was prepared by King Gambhir Singh during his period but completed during the reign of King Chandrakriti.[25] Thus Kalashaya became Bishnupriya in Manipur. In Manipur, Bishnupriyas were completely absorbed as Manpuri in the assimilation process of the Manpuris. So no one could visualize the emerging of concrete solidify group of the Bishnupriya in the social strata of the Manipuris in Manipur. But the same process was not happening to the outside of Manipur where the Kalashaya was settling as sub caste of Bangalli community since time immemorial.

Academic Clarification

Though eminent scholars of Bengali claim Bishnupriyas as Manipuris, maximum academic clarification are being given by the scholars of Manipur. From their statement, the people of this region come to understand that Bishnupriyas are Indo-Aryan and their language belongs to Indo-Aryan whereas the Manipuris belongs to Mongoloid family and their language is Tibeto-Burman in origin. Moreover, the scholars pointed out clearly that when they came to Manipur, where they had been staying and the period in which they returned to outside territories of Manipur. According to Census Report of India and Anthropological Survey of India (ASI), the most authentic report of India, there are 325 languages and 25 scripts.[26] (This report was given by Peoples of India Project (POI) in 1985; further mention was made in K.S. Singh and Manohar's book entitled Language and Script, 1997).[27] According to this book, there are 226 Sino-Tibetan languages (p6), the Manipuri language is also one of them including 31 tribes of Manipur. But the Bishnupriyas were not included and clearly identified as the language belonging to Indo Aryan family.

One pertinent questions which merits discussion is why conflict is going on after maximum academic clarification were and are being made.

After deeply analyzing the issue of Bishnupriya and Manipuri language conflict, we come to understand that the conflict is really a game plan of those scholars who wanted to create an impasse of non-principle antagonistic contradictions among the different communities of North-East India. In other words, they are the architects for internal contradictions with the people of Manipur, who are at stake in the national liberation movement. As cited analogy, mention should be made about the creation of enemies among the people of North East India i.e. Naga vs. Kukis, Arunachali vs. Chakmas. Boro vs. Santhals and Assamese, Meitei vs. Meitei Muslims and Bishnu Priyas and Mizo vs. Riang. This is the easiest and effective method to counter revolutionary movement in North East India known as none military, unarmed counter insurgency operation.[28]

Here, another example could be made that, in the International norms and mechanism of working group of Indigenous peoples, the indigenous peoples of the land has the right to protect their land in order to claim right of the nation to self-determination.[29] In other words, the Manipuris are real indigenous peoples in Manipur (including Meitei Pangals and 33 hill tribes).[30] They have the right to protect their land with the indigenous peoples' understanding of land ownership, not on the basis of colonial interpretation of land. So, they are the owner of land, water and all forms of resources including the flora and fauna. In the case of the Manipuris, it could not be put into practice if some groups strongly claimed that the so called original Manipuris are not aboriginal peoples. The same formula is applied by Bishnupriya under the strong influence of Bengali communities. The Bishnupriyas tried to make confusion to the issue of the Manipuri indegineous identity contending that the Manipuris (present inhabitants of Manipur) are not aboriginal. They dubiously asserted that they are the original settlers of Manipur and that they were driven out from Manipur by the Meiteis in the eighteen centuries. They even claimed that the Manipuri language is for them, neither for the Meeteis nor for the other tribes.

The above ideas are borrowed by the scholars of both Bishnupriya and Bengalis from the incidents of Liberation Tigers of Tamil Elam (LTTE), an organisation which is formed by the ethnic Tamils after migrating from Tamil Nadu. To day, the international communities and international body are still perplexed about the legitimacy of the LTTE's demand for the right to self determination in Sri Lanka after occupying some areas of Sri Lanka. It makes the genuineness of the LTTE's movement meaningless just like a boat without destiny.

The Interest of Third Party in the Conflict:

Mention was made in the foregoing pages that the Bengali scholars and some of the eminent India's agent wanted to make non-principle antagonistic contradiction among the peoples of North East India as internal contradiction. The result is that making the counter part or party of Manipuris is employed by them as means of countering the revolutionary movement. So the Government of India remains silent when Bishnupriya claimed Manipuri as their language, the language which has the status of a scheduled language.[31]

Peoples' Movements in which Direction

From the very beginning, the Manipuris have been reacting against the recognition of Bishnupriya as Bishnupriya Manipuri language in the form of sit-in-protest, Bundh, organizing of public meeting, etc. These are being done by different organizations of Manipur both inside and outside of the land. They are UMA, AAMSU, AMSU, MSF, MNF, Manipur Sahitya Parishad, All Tripura Manipuri Association and Sahitya Parishad of Bangladesh, etc. A good number of memoranda have been sent to the Government of India to take necessary action regarding the recognition of this language as Manipuri by the Government of Assam and Tripura. Recently, different students organisations formed the committee namely "North East Students Co-coordinating Committee on Manipuri Identity" on 5-6-1999 and chalked out many programmes of action including legal fight through High court and Supreme Court.[32]

Recent Development

Maximum effort was also made by the Government of Manipur to drop the prefix and suffix of the term 'Manipuri' to the Bishnupriya. The government representatives met the authority of Central Government, Assam and Tripura to take the necessary action regarding this issue.It can be mentioned that-

i. some opposition party booked public interest litigation to the high court.

ii. Recently the government of Assam has resolved to stop the study of the Bishnupriya-Manipuri in primary school.[33]

What to be Done

People's movement as reaction against the

Bishnupriya issue to keep clear the identity of the Manipuris is the mandate of all. Indication is plenty through press media with many write ups by many individuals. Here the notable thing is that the movement should be based on constructive means, not destructive. The leaders of the movement should be very diplomatic. As far as the movement is continuing on a large scale involving masses, we have to make a touch line with the Bishnupriyas also. We have to identify the third party and their interest, otherwise enmity among us will be inevitable.

The leaders of the movement or concerned people have to make the following programmes and project for them with their participation in the movement. They are given below:

1. Some scholars should be assigned to trace back the real origin of Bishnupriyas and how they are too backward as sub caste of Bengalis.
2. The scholars should publish a good number of Books written about them, not as clarifications of Manipuris and Bishnupriyas conflict.
3. Cultural programmes and book exhibition should be held continuously at frequent intervals in different parts of Assam, Tripura and Bangladesh, where the two communities got settlement.[34]

In short, preventive diplomacy is the best way to resolve the conflict in between Manipuris and Bishnupriyas otherwise it will create great enmities and make the internal contradiction more voluminous. It is suicidal war.

Genesis of Liberation Army (Insurgency) in NE India

The seven states of North East India are not free

from arms action though their people were peace loving in the past. The revolutionary warfare activities in different forms have changed the socio-economic and political outlook of the people living here. Insurgency, termed by the government, has been defined to be the efforts to obtain political goals by an organized group using protracted, irregular warfare and allied political techniques. It is an attempt by military inferior faction (insurgency) operating within a geo-political system by the use of guerrilla warfare and population control measures to usurp the control of system from military faction (*de facto* Government). Further, insurgency is the technique of revolution which combines irregular warfare, political and psychological motivation of the populace, guerrilla tactics and exploitation of deteriorating social and economic conditions. Insurgency has both military and political components.[35]

The area has become the hub of all insurgents' activities in the Northeast for two main reasons. First, because of its strategic location in that it provides militant, a safe passage into Bangladesh. Second, it became a base which provides proximity with all states in the Northeast except in Arunachal Pradesh.

The root of insurgency in this region lies in the economic backwardness as well as political alienation of tribal population from the mainstream of national life. The economic backwardness stems from the unexploited natural resources, inadequate infrastructure, absence of development in tertiary and secondary sectors etc. besides, physiographic constraints, peripheral location, negligence of the region from the very beginning, government apathy towards this region both during pre and post independence period and the result of economic exploitation of the tribals by outsiders. These are the reasons behind revolutionary warfare in this pocket of India.

Physiographic constraints, geographical isolation, peripherialisation of the region yearning communication gap, long years of neglect, indifference of the Nation to the hardship, worries of their compatriots in this strategic region, unimaginative government policies and gross ignorance of the tribal ethos have created among the Tibeto-Burman people a sharp awareness of their ethnic and cultural differences from the national mainstream. They remain drifted rather towards making closer affinities in the Shan and Kachin states of Burma and Bangladesh's Chittagong Hill Tract.

With the rapid rise of money economics, the tribal economy and archaic way of checking out a livelihood have no places in the modern economic race.

Economic hardships due to poor and underdeveloped agriculture, alarming mass unemployment problem, rampant corruption, lack of education and medical facility, exorbitant prices and shortage of essential commodities in the far-flung area of the North East forced the promising youths to come to the path of national liberation movement with arms in Tripura, Assam, Manipur and other states of the region.

Social tension resulting from the tribal feelings of being cornered in their own land caused by dualistic growth of Tripura economy during the last one hundred years, scarcity of flat land fit for wet cultivation where the tribal Jhumias could easily rehabilitated, exploitation of rural tribals by non-tribals (mostly Bengalees) and other merchants have created complex problem of social inequality. Tribals in Tripura have been marginalized and far behind in secondary and tertiary sectors.[36]

Peripheral location, geographical isolation,[37] land locked character of Northeast India are facing not so friendly countries.[38] Like Bangladesh, Burma and China and a prorupt shape due to protrusion of Bangladesh have a great geo-political significance in the domain of insurgency. It plays a pivotal role in escalating extremist activities.

Besides economic hardships, physiographic constraints, geographical isolation and cultural diversity, one could not discard their historical legacy and its importance. It is not a law and order problem and it should not be conceived that it is due to unemployment and misleading of all. It is the distorted perception in the form of official projections of Government and a handful of intellectuals. In reality, it is a contradiction of re-colonisation and decolonisation by having deep organisational class structure of the oppressed people. As a consequence, there is class struggle in between the oppressed and the oppressor. It is being sustained by historical legacy and its importance. Historical evidences are that (i) Manipur and Tripura had been annexed to the Indian Political fold, after two years of Indian independence; (ii) Assam became a part of British-India not by her choice, but by the agreement bnetween Burma and the British, who signed the Treaty of Yandaboo in 1826; (iii) the ethnic tribes who remained in the excluded hill areas of Assam fused themselves in the last five decades into nationhood and claimed independence prior to the passage of Indian Independence Act 1947.

So, the Government should give proper answers of this historical legacy and its importance which is always associated with the political discourse of decolonisation.

Unfortunately, the other Indians could not realise the genuine problems and the years of neglect of North-East India. It is, however, acknowledged by the militants who have already drifted away from the mainstream and demanded to have their own political status. But the question is "Can the Delhi Government's compensation for the injustice done by them all these decades eliminate the political aspiration and firm determination of many young people, who have sacrificed their lives for the better future of their masses in the region?" No one desires to have the relationship in between two states like mammon and ragamuffin.

NOTES AND REFERENCES

1. *Freedom*, vol.4, issue 3 February 2001.
2. *Freedom,* vol.5, issue 15 July 2002.
3. *Memorandum* submitted by the RPF to the Chairman, Decolonization Committee, United Nations 11 December 1996, p.XV.
4. Report of the Commission of Inquiry on Assam Disturbances, 1983, Tribhuvan Prasad Tewary Chairman, May 1984, Dispur, Assam.
5. The American Senate provides equal representation to the states. This right is extended to the states which joined later, but were not original contracting parties. Equal representation was also given to the constituent states in the House of Nationalities of the former Soviet Union. If equal representation is given to the states, irrespective of whether they are big or small in the Council, the small states will have a legitimate interest. And which will satisfy to a great extent the sentiments of the small states and they will feel that they are equal partners in shaping the future of the country. Until and unless it has been done, there will always be a tendency to separate from the Indian Union.
6. Prafulla Misra, Insurgency in NE Region and Malaise in the System, in the book, *Insurgency in NE India*, New Delhi, 1997, p.204.

7. Prof. Naorem Sanajaoba, Armed Forces Special Powers Act, 1958, in eds., S. Bhubol, *The Orient Vision,* Vol.2 issue 1, Oct.-Nov.-Dec., 2004, p.3. Also see his media features since 1997.
8. B.S. Burtola, Development Discourses in Social Sciences Research in the NE Region,eds., Bimal Deb, *Development Priorities in NE India,* New Delhi, 2002, p.164.
9. MASS, Human Rights Violation in Assam, cited in Sanajaoba's Naoriya 'Human Rights', Delhi, 1994, p139.
10. *Human Right violation,* Compiled for private circulatulation by Committee on Human Rrights (COHR), Imphal.
11. R. Gopalkrishnan, *The North-East India- Land, Economy and People,* Delhi, 1995, p.145.
12. *Ibid.*, 146.
13. *People's Democracy*, December 1, 2002.
14. The Assam Tribune, Guwahati, 23 January 19 97,
15. *Op.cit.*, March 21, 2004.
16. *Ibid.*
17. *Ibid.*
18. *Ibid.*
19. *Ibid.*
20. Sabri Bandy Padhyay' "Migration in the North Eastern Region of India in the perspective of Security and Development, eds., S.K. Agnihotri & B. Datta Ray, *Perspective of Security and Development in NE India*, Concept Publishing, New Delhi, 2005, p.164.
21. Kailash Sarma, Population Growth and Demographic Balance in NE in the Threshold of the New Millennium" eds., Bimol J Dab, *Development Priorities in NE India,* New Delhi, 2002, p.164. Also see The Hindustan Times, *NGO Report on Illigal Migrants in Assam,* New Delhi, May 15, 2002.
22. Rafiul Ahmed, Prasenjit Biswas, *Political Economy of Underdeveopment of North East India*, Akansha Publishing House, New Delhi, 2004, Pp.63-64.
23. *Ibid.*
24. *Ibid.*
25. O. Bogeshor, eds., *Sanamahi Laikan (Manipuri chronicle)* Imphal, dt. not cited.

26. *The Census Report of India and Anthropological Survey of India (ASI), 1997. The Peoples of India Project (POI), 1985.*
27. K.S. Singh & Manohar, *Language and Script*, 1997, p.6.
28. AMUCO, *7th Integrity Day Souvenir*, Imphal: 4 August 2004, pp.171 & 197.
29. Draft United Nations Declaration on the Rights of Indigenous Peoples (Art 3), *AITPN Report 2003.*
30. Recommendations of Seminar organised by Centre for Progress of Manipuri People Imphal: Kuki Inn, 30 & 31 May 1997.
31. Interview with Kamlakanta from Silchar, Social Activist on 13 Feb. 1998, Silchar.
32. Statement given by Ng. Modhuchandra, the President of UMA (United Manipur Association) in the discussion on the theme, "Integrity and Identity of the Global Manipuri to Enhance the Cause of World Peace" organised by the UMA at Silchar, 22 June 2003.
33. Information given by Ngangom Ramakanta, Secretary, COPIN, Committee on Culture for Peace and Integrity, Silchar, 25 Feb., 2005.
34. Suggestion given by Eminent Scholar of NE, Prof. N. Sanajaoba Sixth Annual Session of United Manipuri Association (UMA), at Bathdurgwas in Cachar, on 12 Feb., 1998.
35. Thompson, Robert, *Defeating Communist Insurgency*, London 1996 as cited in International Terrorism: a kind of conflict, Delhi, p.64.
36. S.N.Singh, Kumar Amarendra Narain, *Northeast Insurgency*, Delhi, 1997, as cited in Insurgency in North East India, p.200.
37. Border line and the length (roughly) between: Assam – Bhutan 500 km, Arunachal Pradesh–China 117 km, AP–Burma 525 km, Bangladesh–Assam 200 km, Manipur–Burma 425 km, Mizoram–Bangladesh 275 km, Tripura–Bangladesh 625 km, Meghalaya–Bangladesh 400 km, (Total: 4825 km excluding Sikkim).
38. Bhattacharjee, PR, *Economic Transition in Tripura*, Delhi, 1993, p.33.

3

GUERRILLA ACTION OF MAJOR INSURGENT GROUPS

The North-East, too, remained an occupied part and parcel of the semi-colonial and semi feudal Indian society. The Nehru government at the centre installed by the British continued the colonial legacy of national subjugation and followed such policies so as to strengthen the existing backward pre-capitalist production-relations in this region belying the patriotic and democratic hopes and aspirations of the common masses of various nationalities. As a result, the economy of this region remained intact in the hands of the imperialists, the comprador bourgeoisie and the big landlords.

Further, as part of the imperialist policy of appropriating maximum and quick profit, the government handed over the entire trade and commerce and small-scale industrial sector of the region to the rich businessmen from outside the region thus depending on the local nascent commercial bourgeois class. Even the administrative posts were filled up by personnel from outside the region which only fuelled national frustration and the sense of national deprivation among the growing middle classes of various oppressed nationalities. Along with their economic factors, the suppression of native languages and culture by the imposition of English, Hindi and other developed languages further alienated the relatively small and backward nationalities from the relatively big and developed nationalities of the region there by giving rise to several language movements during the last decades in all states of the region.

Thus, the problem of nationality in the NE has assumed quite a complex dimension as a result of glaringly uneven economic, political and cultural development of the region's inhabitants. The problem has become exorbitant. The problem has become more complicated with the failure of successive governments in tackling all these discontentment of the people.

Therefore, the sense of negligence and deprivation developed by non-privileged groups found expression, often in the forums of national country, the feeling of deprivation is found almost in all of its regions and sections of population. It may however be noted that the discontent of secessionist type is mostly found in its frontier regions or peripheries such as the Tamils in the South, the Akalis and the Kashmiris in the North, and a large section of people in the entire Northeastern region. The different ethnic groups of this region have been complaining of being deprived of what they call "Legitimate Share" of national wealth and political power by the dominant section of the population.[1] In view of this, some of them have been fighting for the right to self determination and others, launching movements for the creation of separate states, while some others are pressing for special constitutional safeguards of their respective identities.

Most of the nationalities of Northeast Region have always been on the fringe of the rest of the country. Administratively, it was never a part of India till the advent of the British although there were influences of Indian culture over some of its areas. Due to obvious reasons, this region was not sufficiently integrated by the British with the rest of the country. Even during the last four and a half decades of independence, diverse groups of these regions could not be brought into the mainstream of national culture and character. As a result, different nationalities of this region have always been feeling a sense of alienation. More important, some sections of these groups have been involving in armed struggle in a bid to establish a sovereign independent state of their respective areas outside the Indian Union. Thus the insurgency movements have been launched by the good numbers of organizations.[2] The list of organisations which are declared as outlawed by the Unlawful Activities Ordinance, 2004 issued by the Government of India (GOI) are as follows:

1. Barbar Khalsa International
2. Khalistan Commando Force
3. Khalistan Zindabad Force
4. International Sikh Youth Federation
5. Lashkar-E-Taiba/Pasban-E-Ahle Hadis
6. Jaish-E Mohammed/Tahrik-E-Ahle Hadis
7. Harkat-Ul-Mujahideen/Harkat-Ul-Ansar/Harkat-Ul-Jehad-E-Islami.
8. Hizb-Ul-Mujahideen/Hizb-Ul-Mujahideen Pir Panjal Regiment.
9. Al-Umar-Mujahideen.
10. Jammu and Kashmir Islamic Front.

11. United Liberation Front of Assam (ULFA)
12. National Democratic Front of Bodoland(NDFB)
13. People's Liberation Army(PLA)
14. United National Liberation Front (UNLF)
15. People's Revolutionary Party of Kangleipak (PREPAK)
16. Kangleipak Communist Party (KCP)
17. Kanglei Yaol Kanba Lup (KYKL)
18. Manipur People's Liberation Front (MPLF)
19. All Tripura Tiger Force
20. National Liberation Front of Tripura
21. Liberation Tigers of Tamil Eelam (LTTE)
22. Students Islamic Movement of India
23. Deendar Anjuman
24. Communist Party of India (Marxist-Leninist) People's War

    All its formations and front Organisations.
25. Maoist Communist Centre (MCC), All Its Formations And Front Organisation
26. Al Badr
27. Jamiat-Ul-mujahidden
28. Al-qaida
29. Dukhtaran-E-millat (DEM)
30. Tamil Nadu Liberation Army (TNLA)
31. Akhil Bharat Nepali Ekta Samaj (ABNES)

Among them, the major organisations operating in the North East are those which are given in the bold letter in the names given above. The major organisations are fighting for national liberation while the lesser ones are ethnic army to protect the interest of their ethnic groups and demanded autonomy.[3] Some major organisations of each state need to be discussed along with their historical importance.

Guerrilla Action and National Liberation Movement in Manipur

The history of Manipur is little known to other Indians. Manipur has a recorded history of its own and it dates back to AD 33, when Nongda Lairen Pakhangba ascended the throne as the first feudal lord of Manipur.[4] Loyamba, one of the wisest and ablest kings of Manipur ascended the throne in AD 1074. He wrote the *Loiyumba Sinlon*, the first written constitution of Manipur. "The book (*Loiyumba Sinlon*) deals with the Rules and Regulations governing the customs, duties, etiquettes etc., of the officers and the common people among the Meeteis from the fifth century". Manipur had 74 kings since AD 33 till 55.[5] The annexation of Manipur in 1891 to the British India Empire put an end to the Monarchy in Manipur. In place of this a Durbar was constituted with limited legislative and judiciary powers. According to Prof. Sanajaoba Naoriya, an eminent scholar of NE, the sovereignty of Manipur was honoured by the British crown even after its defeat in the Anglo-Manipuri War, 1891.[6] When all the powerful historical kingdoms in the Indian Subcontinent fell flat like, a house of cards and easily annexed to the British Empire even without a grumble, such events did not happen in the case of Manipur.[7] The British gobbled up all the powerful Indian kingdoms except Manipur and Tripura among others, which it honoured for its valor. The Government of India following hectic debates about Manipur in the British Parliament proclaim:

> *"It is further notified that the Majesty the Queen, Empress of India, has been pleased to forgo Her right to annex Her Indian Dominions the territories of the Manipur State; and has graciously assented to the re-establishment of Native Rule under such conditions as the Governor-General in Council may consider desirable . . ."*

In the words of Barrister M.M. Ghose, Manipur was already an Asiatic Sovereign, which had its native rule continued till its merger into the Indian Union in 1949. The external sovereignty partly eroded as the Britishers deputed a political agent to look after British interest in Manipur and outside; at most British had limited suzerainty over Manipur to some extent without affecting the native rule. Although the British political agent exercised considerable power, a historian clearly defines its political status; "It is quite evident that the duty of the Political Agent in Manipur was like that of an ambassador". Sometimes ambassadors could be more powerful considering the international or bilateral relations. What is important to historians is not how strong and influential was the Political Agent but is how far its master, the British Crown honors the native rule by Meetei kings.[8]

Prior to the merger, the Maharaja of Manipur ruled under "Rules for the Management of the state of Manipur", which was enforced on 14 September, 1933, the enabling Article 1 of the 1935 Rules states:

> *"His Highness the Raja will be responsible for the administration of the state, He will be assisted by a Durbar which will consist of an officer specially selected by the Governor of Assam who will be styled as the President and at least three Manipuri Members . . ."*

They merely assisted the Manipur Monarch and responsibility did not lie with his assistants.

Manipur State Constitution Act (here state implies Nation-State) empowers the Maharaja in Council to administer the state thereby installing a 'constitutional monarchy' following the model of the British Crown, subject to numerous checks and balances. Article 3 of the Act provides, "Government of the state by His Highness, the Maharaja: The territories for the time being and hereafter vested in the Maharaja are governed by and in the name of the Maharaja All rights, authority and jurisdiction which appertain or are incidental to the Government of such territories are provision of this Act".[9] The entire Manipuri Constitution could be amended following the due procedure for constitutional amendment. This sufficiently indicates the Manipuri political culture which could keep pace with the democratic aspirations of the incoming civilizations, should such dynamic and progressive and political ethos be contained in totalitarian system with a rigid constitution nearing a closed system, like the Indian Constitution, it should be like showing hospitality to the aquatic lives in the beautiful expanses of a desert. The rigid structure of dominance which is a logical extension of casteism, is completely foreign to Meetei mental make-up and when the casteists throw their casteist glance and manners, the Meeteis simply conceive the ethos as pre-historic gestures. Similar is the case with a constitution.

With the consolidation of a newly born Indian Union, Manipur was brought within the fold of the Union after the signing by the representatives of the two Governments, of the instrument of merger on September 21, 1949. The merger was not a smooth sailing business and later on, it became a curious object or controversy, since Manipur had a history of independence, a constitutional monarchy preceded by governments under 'Rule of law' and had experienced as to how to meet the challenge of the mighty British Crown at the peak of its power and had also taken up armed struggle three years after the World War II which had its operational theatre in itself.[10] When one became weary of the successive events of war including the seven years-devastation by the Burmese in early nineteenth century, the merger was signed by a Maharaja under duress, which was not ratified by the Maharaja in council or by the legislature. The general feeling is that a constitutional head, which had political obligation to a constitution, lacked the political capacity to sign all instrument of merger in the absence of ratification by the constitutionally elected assembly and a plebiscite.

The Maharaja was concerned to sign the Instrument of Accession on August 11, 1947 under which Defence, Communication, External relations passed within the exclusive jurisdiction of New Delhi. Prior to the merger on October 15 1949 as a response to the pressure from the officials of New Delhi, the Maharaja clarified that he was governed by the Manipuri Constitution, unlike other rulers of the native kingdoms. He wrote to the concerned official of Government of India on September 20, 1949, just one day before he was coerced to put his signature to the merger agreement. The letter states:

> *"Direct dealing with me was feasible when sovereignty was vested in me but, after the introduction of the State Constitution Act, the Sovereignty and administration of the State has been shifted to the people."*

Earlier, the Maharaja wrote to the official of Government of India "if I am compelled to work independently of my people my action will be quite unjustifiable".[11] He also wrote three days before to the official of government of India, "Now that the sovereignty of the state has been vested in the people. It would be in the fitness of things to hear the people's voice and learn their sentiment so that the line of action may not in any case be unconstitutional".[12] In the fitness of things, a referendum on merger could have been held, but the colonial chieftains had not taught their greedy political heirs what constitutional procedure should have to be followed short of confiscating the state by war, even at the peak of power, the mighty British Crown had foregone even their right to annexation of Manipur after a state of belligerency in 1891 and through debate in the Parliament.

Here one could raise a question that why the story of merger agreement is stressing up and down again and again. The answer is that it is the only argument made by all the militant groups of Manipur. Even they claimed that Manipur was an occupied territory of India and deploying security forces of India was named as occupying forces. They considered it as a hidden war of India against the Manipuris by snatching their sovereignty. So, waging war against India means war against war. It means that they are compelled to launch armed resistance in order to restore the lost sovereignty of Manipur. So it is true to say that the armed struggle started by Irawat from the latter part of 1948 and formation of Meitei State committee in 1960, United National Liberation Front (UNLF) in 1964 and People Liberation Army (PLA) in 1978 are having the same argument and aspiration. But notable thing is that Irawat started armed struggle from 1948 which continued upto 1951, UNLF from 1991 and PLA from its formation (1978).[13]

Liberation Army (Insurgency of Manipur)

The British departed on 14 August and the Manipuris hoisted the Pafan flag' (it is a national flag of Manipur having picture of Pakhangba in a snake form) at 10 o'clock and 15 minutes A.M. at the same day at Kangla. Fourteenth August is the independence day of Manipur.[14] Towards the end of 1948, Manipur became a constitutional monarchy with a legislative Assembly consisting of 53 members including 18 hill men. It was dissolved after the annexation of Manipur to India and a Chief Commissioner took over its administration. In it, there was no Manipur Assembly because of its part C state status. It was the same administration of the British by sending their political agent to Manipur. Such step-motherly treatment of the centre was severely criticized by some educated youths of Manipur. With this view in their minds, they formed the "United National Liberation Front" (UNLF) under the leadership of Arambam Somorendra to achieve what they called the "right to national self determination" and fight for an independent Manipur on 24 November 1964. Most of its members were highly educated youths. This was the first powerful underground organization set up after the death of Hijam Irabot with an avowed aim to liberate Manipur and other Indo-Burma (Myanmar) region (the north eastern part of India and north western part of Myanmar). They followed the socialistic pattern of society.

Within a few years of UNLF's existence, some militant members of the UNLF including Oinam Sudhir and Nameirakpam Bisheshwar had different views with the founder of the organisation on some issues. While Bisheshwar and Sudhir wanted immediate armed revolution, Somorendra preferred to postpone it. So in 1960, Sudhir set up "Revolutionary Government of

Manipur" (RGM) at Sylhet and printed pamphlets to be circulated in Imphal. He emerged as a powerful leader of CONSCOM and RGM but his dictatorial attitude his organization was not lasting. Bisheshwar also formed another revolutionary organisation known as People's Liberation Army (Eastern region) in 1978. It became one of the most powerful armed groups in North Eastern India after 1981 because of its attack against the security forces with arms and tried to consolidate the people of North East.[15] But Central Committee of the UNLF in a booklet circulated in Imphal valley on the occasion of 27th anniversary of its exsistence, declared the launching of an armed struggle on 24th November 1991 for achieving an independent Manipur.[16]

Besides these two organizations, there are other insurgent groups. They are People's Revolutionary Party of Kangleipak (PREPAK), Kangleipak Communist Party (KCP) and Kanglei Yaon Kanna Lup (KYKL). They are attacking against the security forces, police informants and commit extortions. The there groups, RPF, UNLF and PREPAK, are reported to have come together with interest to form an umbrella organisation for intensifying insurgency. It was called as MPLF (Manipur People's Liberation Front). The Kanglei Yaon Kanna Lup (KYKL) led by Oken, a faction from UNLF is taking 'Operation New Kangleipak' to clean up the education system in the state.

Recently, RK Sanayaima @ Meghen, Chairman of UNLF reacted to the Republic Day Speech of the Governor, S.S. Sidhu this year (2005). The proscribed UNLF said that in order to find a lasting solution to the Indo-Manipur conflict, the root cause should be first understood and spelt out a four joint proposal for the Government of India to ponder over.

In a statement issued to press on Feb. 3, 2005, Chairman of the outfit, Sana Yaima said that the main root of conflict is the independence of Manipur. "As such it is necessary to seek the mandate of the people by holding a plebiscite under the United Nations".

To make the plebiscite free and fair, UNLF proposed that the services of the UN peace keeping force be utilized. Further, it states: "to enable the plebiscite to be held within the time frame given by the UN, the cadres of UNLF will deposit their arms with the UN Peace keeping Force. Similarly, the Indian Government should withdraw its regular army and para military forces from Manipur"[17]

As far as peace talk is concerned, Irengbam Chaoren, Chairman of RPF and its armed wing PLA stated on the 'Independence Demand Day' of his party on 25th Feb. 2005 that it should be decided by the people. The party would observe the response of the Government of India and his organisation will not deposit their arms to any group.ThePLA is the only organisation in North East to become signatory of the Geneva Convention common Article 3 and his organisation submitted memorandum to the Chairman of Decolonisation Committee of UN in 1996.

The memorandum was submitted by the organisation on behalf of all the dependent and colonized people of Manipur representing the ethnic and indigenous people, namely, the Meeteis, the Nagas, the Kukis-Chins for granting and restoration of independence and decolonisation of the State of Manipur from the present colonial and hegemonic Administrative Power of India.

They had submitted six prayers with historical facts, political, socio-economic materials as well as legal and constitutional materials. They are as follows:

1. for maintaining, supervising and examining historical materials/records;
2. for terminating the foreign and colonial regime of the aforesaid Administrative Power;
3. for international appraisal annexation of the Nation-State of Manipur in 1949 A.D. and the suspended/ subservient sovereignty thenceforth;
4. for giving international recognition to the national liberation movement of Manipur, which continues since the time of annexation in 1949 till today, and
5. for all necessary ad elaborate steps, appropriate measures towards complete de-colonisation of Manipur and cessation of subjugation of its people to the earliest, and lastly, for holding emergent as well as subsequent sessions of the De-colonisation Committee in Imphal City, the capital of Manipur, considering the massive army occupation of the state and repressive laws of the state, which prevent any sort of physical and material representation of the national liberation movement to the UN and the concerned international bodies.

ULFA and UNLF signed a deal for joint operation. Soon after UNLF claimed responsibility for the July 16, 2002, killing of 3 Jat Regiment soldiers in Assam's Cachar district. UNLF and PLA's main area of operation is Manipur's Jiribam valley and Cachar. In the recent past, a unified command of MPLF enduringly engaged with the Border Security Force in a gun-fight for four days in which the later had to withdrew without attaining any significant result. It is a real progress of the story of their armed struggle after the demise of Somorendra of UNLF and Bisheshwar of PLA. But, of late no such report of joint operations were forthcoming. At present, the leaders of these two organisations are R.K. Meghen and Chaoren.

Nagaland

In 1942, the Naga leader, Z.A. Phizo, moved to Burma with his followers with an ambition to create an independent nation of the Nagas, and established contact with the Japanese. In 1945, the Nagas submitted a memorandum to J.P. Mills, advisor to the Governor for Tribal Affairs, stating that they did not want to be part of a free India and would like to remain as British subjects. The Naga National Council (NNC) was formed with a demand for autonomy within the Assamese administration stated in 1947 expressing that they were willing to accept India's Sovereignty for 10 years after which they should have the right of self-determination. But in 1975 Shillong Accord was made in order to bring peace. The insurgents surrendered their weapons and accepted the state of Nagaland within the Indian Union.

NSCN was formed on 31st January 1980 by Issak Chisi Swu, Thuingaleng Muivah and S.S. Khaplang opposing the 'Shillong Accord' signed by the NNC with the Indian government. Since then it has been carrying on an armed struggle to bring an end to Indian Sovereignty over the Naga people and establish a People's Republic of Nagaland. The Indian government's persistent efforts to start a dialogue process created differences among the leadership of NSCN and this disagreement took its toll on the organisation. On 30th April 1988, after an attempt to assassinate Muivah failed, in which several cadres were killed, the NSCN split into two factions, namely the NSCN led by S.S. Khaplang, NSCN (K), and the NSCN led by Issak and Muivah, NSCN (IM). The former suspected Issak and Muivah of secretly initiating talks with the Indian government.

All the two groups have headquarters in Myanmar, and training camps in the Chittagong Hills of Bangladesh and Arakan and some Somra Hills of Myanmar. They have links with the Karen and Kachin rebels of Myanmar. NSCN groups have links with the ULFA and Bodo rebels. But that is not cordial after it claimed directly greater Nagaland by embracing the surrounding areas from Manipur, Assam and Arunachal Pradesh.

The government of India has a talk with NSCN groups, which is frequently violated by them. Th. Muivah was arrested by the Thailand police in January, 2000 for traveling on forged documents. He was released a few months later but directed not to leave Thailand. Meanwhile, the government continues talks with him, but today he got India's passport and recently came to Delhi and his homeland Nagaland as part of Indo-Naga peace talk.

Tripura

The insurgency in Tripura has grown out of conflicts between the Tripuri natives and immigrants. Bengalis' dominance in jobs, commerce and business was resented by the Tripuri natives, and the influx of refugees from East-Pakistan after independence has also inflamed the situation. In 1967, the Tripura Upjati Juba Samiti (TUSS) was formed to demand restoration of indigenous Tripuris' lands in possession of the Bengali immigrants and the East Pakistani foreigner, autonomous district councils for the Tripuri natives, reservation of government jobs for them, and recognition of Kok-Barak as the official state language. Militants among the TUSS formed an underground organization, Tripura National Volunteers (TNV). During 1979-1987, there were militant attacks on police station; markets were looted and public property of Bengali destroyed. In 1988, a tripartite agreement was signed between the central and state governments and TNV, under which TNV was to abandon its secessionist policy and violence, and the surrendering insurgents were to be rehabilitated Peace lasted for 3 years. In February, 1991, a new militant outfit, National Liberation Front of Tripura (NLFT), attacked the Jainani Police outpost, and violence has since continued. In 1997, there were 303 violent incidents and 270 people were killed, including 50 security- personnel.

In 1998, there were 568 incidents, with 250 persons killed, including 25 security personnel. In the first 9 months of 1999, there were 455 violent incidents claiming 181 lives, including 25 security personnel. There are 12 active insurgent groups in Tripura, NMLFT and ATTF (All Tripura Tiger Force) being the most dangerous. All have their bases in the Chittagong Hills of Bangladesh for training hideouts and buying arms. Attacks on security personnel, non-tribals, mostly Bengalis, and extortions are their main activities. For full understanding of their unrest and uprising of Tripuras, we need to stretch full details of it.

Tripuris' Unrest and Uprising

The indigenous Tripuris of Tripura have been harbouring great discontent against the immigrants for a long time past and this discontentment persists even today mainly because of the large-scale economic exploitations carried out by the non-tribes specially the Bengali Hindus. Thus the settlement of the Bengalees under the patronage of the Tripura Kings proved disastrous to the subsistence economy of the tribes although the objective was good enough for the development of both the state and the tribes themselves. The Tripura kings could not realise that large-scale settlement of the Bengalees and granting of all sorts of privileges would later have a disastrous effect on the interests and welfare of the indigenous tribes. It was rather the Tripuri natives who started realizing that their economic interests were being seriously hampered by the settlement of the Bengalees coming from outside the state. This created a bad feeling of discontent and distrust between the two well before India attained independence in 1947. It was the last ruling Raja Bir Bikram Kishroe (1923-47) who ultimately realised the situation and made decisions to reserve an area of 1950 sq. miles of fertile lands for the five indigenous tribes of Triprua as already stated earlier.

Realising the prevailing discontent and distrust among the people, some progressive-minded youths formed a popular organisation in 1937 known as the Tripura Rajya Janamangal Samity. The second organization known as the Tripura Rajya Gana Parishad was also formed by the Congress-minded youths soon thereafter. The two organizations started their movements with the demands accompanied with some violent expressions. But the outbreak of the Second World War led to the suppression of their movements by the British Government. After the War the Janamanghal Samity was dissolved and a new organisation known as the Tripura Rajya Praja Mandal was formed in its stead by the members of the Communist Party of India. The Maharaja Bir Bikram did not recognize this organisation but he could not do anything before his death in May 1946 except to decide for accession of his state to the proposed Indian Union on attaining its independence the following year.

Immediately after Independence of India, a huge waves of foreigners immigrated from East Pakistan to Tripura due to the partition of the country when the starving and famine-striken Tripuri native peasants rose in revolt in what was known as the Golaghati Tripuri Revolt of 1948. The state administration ruthlessly suppressed the movement while giving the East Pakistani foreigners rehabilitation and settlements at the cost of the Tripuri natives. Both the Praja Mandal and the Rajya Gana Parishad continued the resistance movement for the safety and security of the lives and property of the tribes. The situation became so grave that the Government of India was compelled to take over the administration.

The formal integration of Tripura with the Indian Union was completed but no step was taken up to solve the problems of the indigenous settlers of the state; hence the unrest of the Tripuri natives was persecuted and they organised themselves into their own political parties notably the Tripura Upajatai Juba Samiti (TUJS) to look after their own interest and with the objective of restoring an independent state of Tripura. As against this objective of the Tripura natives, a chauvinistic political organisation known as Amra Bangali was formed being patronized by Ananda-Margis. Thus two communal organizations which were diametrically opposite to each other, came into existence in Tripura. Meanwhile the Left Front came into power in Tripura in 1978.

As the native economy became shattered, the Tripuri natives have been deprived of their land-holdings and reduced to servitude working as serfs for their immigrant money-lenders and landholders. With the merger of the State with the Union of India, nothing concrete was done to mitigate the grievances of the tribes and to improve their socio-economic conditions. Hence, the continued and persistent discontent of the tribes and their hatred and anger against the Bengali and East Pakistani foreignes snon-tribes have taken violent turns in recent years. Bijoy Hrankhwal, the Assistant Secretary of the TUJS came into contact with Laldenga of the Mizo National Front (MNF), went underground, formed the Tribal National Volunteers (TNV) and became its supreme commander. Prior to this, Hrangkhwal formed the Tripura Sena as a militia wing of the TUJS. Subsequently, all members of the sena joined the TNV. It was in August 1979, within seven months of its formation, that the TNV in collaboration with the MNF insurgents, started attacking the non-tribals of Tripura. The terror of the tribals on the non-tribals reached its climax on June 6, 1980 at Mandai village in West Tripura district where more than 200 persons were brutally killed. The then Chief Minister of Tripura stated that the main objective of the mass killing was to terrorise the Bengali population to leave Tripura while Bhattacharyya (1991) said that the Mandai Massacre was "only the first milestone of the long distant target".

Meanwhile the CPI(M) Government under the leadership of the Chief Minister Nripen Chakraborty realised the problems of the Tripuri natives and sympathetically decided to establish a Tribal Autonomous Council for them and passed the Tripura Tribal Areas Autonomous District Council Bill, 1979. Now this Act sought to create an autonomous tribal region comprising 7132.56 sq.kms. out of a total of 10,447 sq.kms. being the area of the State and which will be governed by an elected Council composed of 21 tribal and 7 non-tribal members. All the tribes welcomed the move of the State Government but the TUJS and the militants demanded that such an

Autonomous District Council should have been created under the Sixth Schedule of the Indian Constitution. On the other hand, the Amra Bangali called for a Tripura Bandh in January 1980 to register its protest against the Act. But the State Government was firm enough and at the same time arrested Bijoy Hrangkhwal on 13 June, 1980 immediately after the Mandai Massacre. But owing to public demand coming from the tribes, he was released later. The Chief Minister tried hard to win him over but Hrangkhwal was unconvinced and he rather took a more radical step by forming a parralel Government which is called the People's Democratic Republic of Tripura with himself as its President. He declared that people who migrated to Tripura after 15 October 1949 should be treated as foreigners or aliens.

In the meantime, the Central Government constituted a committee on 8 July 1980 after the Mandai massacre under the chairmanship of Shri Dinesh Singh M.P. and former Union Minister of External Affairs and six other members. Among many other things, the committee recommended in a short-term measure, that in view of the disruption of the Autonomous District Council Act passed by the State legislature in 1979 a Planning and implementation Advisory Committee be appointed to review all plans for economic and social development of the tribal areas. The committee shall be presided over by the Chief Minster himself and all Tripuri MLAs and technical and other experts shall be its members. Other important recommendations of the Committee included the proposals for setting up of a Paper Mill in Tripura and a North East Industrial Corporation. It is surprising that the recommendations did not speak about the Autonomous District Council for being brought under the Sixth Schedule. The Indian media has consistently subjugated the Tripuri movement by dubiously projecting the Tripuri-East Pakistani issue as tribal versus non-tribal issue.

Notwithstanding the Dinesh Singh Committee recommendations, the law and order situations of the State deteriorated to a point that a central team had to be sent to Agartala at the end of 1986. By this time, the Tripura Autonomous District Council was already brought under the Sixth Schedule through a Constitutional (49th Amendment) Act 1984. The Central Team held a meeting with Nirpen Chakraborty the then CPI(M) Chief Minister and it was agreed among all those present in the meeting to combat the extremists. But the Chief Minister refused to accept a proposal to extend the Disturbed Areas Act and to ban the TNV on the ground that such measures would place the son of the soils at the mercy of the army. As if to reciprocate, the TNV leadership also changed their strategy by stopping the massacre of the immigrants but resorting to selective killings.

As the Assembly elections in Tripura were due in 1988, the Central Government at the instance of the Prime Minister Rajiv Gandhi, declared the whole State of Tripura as a disturbed area and inducted the armed forces in a massive scale to combat the TNV menace. It was a double-edged sword. It put the Left Front Government to a great disadvantage and made Bijoy Hrangkhawl smell trouble. About a year earlier Hrangkhwl had already addressed a letter to the Prime Minister Rajiv Gandhi hailing him as a great [illegible]. The Left Front lost the election and the Congress (I)-TUJS coalition Government came to power. The guerilla activities of the TNV extremists also stopped. After several rounds of secret negotiations and discussions, a tripartite agreement was struck whereby a Memorandum of Understanding (MoU) was signed on 12 August 1988 between the TNV on the one hand and the Central and the State Governments on the other.

The MoU contains seven important clauses: (i) Deposit of arms and ending of underground activities by TNV, (ii) Rehabilitation of the TNV undergrounds, (iii) Measures to prevent further Infiltration into Tripura, (iv) Reservation of seats in the Tripura Legislative Assembly for Tribals, (v) Restoration of Alienated Lands of Tribals, (vi) Redrawing of the Boundaries of the Autonomous District Council Area, and (vii) Measures for Long Term Economic Development of Tripura.

Implementation of the Peace Accord

Of the Seven Clauses of the Tripura Peace Accord (MoU) signed 15 years ago on 12 August 1988 in New Delhi, the first, the second and the fourth clauses have been implemented without any difficulty. But the remaining fur clauses have not yet been fully implemented. The third clause of the Accord relating to Prevention of Infiltration can be implemented only with better patrolling and vigil of the international border accompanied with the sincere and strict enforcement of the Foreigners Act, 1946. The issue of Bangladeshi infiltration is quite alarming even now in all the Seven States of North East India particularly Assam and Tripura. The MPs from the region had in recent time raised the issue on the floor of Parliament and pointed out the Bangladeshis used the North East Region as a corridor to infiltrate and then spread across the country to create the socio-economic and political problems with implied threat perception. The menace of infiltration of illegal migration will persist until the authorities both at the Centre and in the North eastern states take sincere and vigorous action in the matter. The infiltrators know well the weaknesses of the border security of India and are easily criss-crossing the international borders into India.

The restoration of alienated lands to the indigenous tribals of Tripura as provided in Clause 5 of the Accord could not be implemented satisfactorily because of the stiff opposition put up by the immigrant non-tribals and the softness of the State Government towards the latter. As regards redrawing of the boundaries of Autonomous District Council Area under Clause 6, the implementation was once completed but the immigrant non-tribal demanded that fresh redrawing should be done as they infiltrate into the area of the A.D.C. and the State Government appears to be inclined to keeping the issue alive.

The last Clause No.7 contains seven sub-clauses which have not been fully fulfilled. The last sub-clause speaks about efforts to be made for effective implementation of the provisions of the Sixth Schedule to the Constitution in so far as it relates to the Autonomous District Council in Tripura. The job of the Members of the District Council is subjected to sincere support and cooperation of both the State and Central Governments.[18]

Assam

It is really strange to the people of mainland India that Assam is in touch with violent rebellion and was always regarded as part of the Indian 'national mainstream', also witnessed insurgency with the rise of the United Liberation Front of Assam (ULFA), which pledged armed struggle for independence. The organisation has some setback under sustained military operation in 1991, but is regrouping in Bangladesh and in parts of Assam.18 A question, hereby, could be arisen why the Assamese had been launching such separatist movement with arms. The Assamese were ailed after Bengali was introduced as the official language of the province in 1937. Assam Sangrakshini Sabha, formed in 1926 and renamed as Ahom Jatiya Mahasabha submitted a memorandum on January 26, 1946 to the British Parliamentary Delegation, that 'Assam for the Assamese is the battle cry of all the true sons of Assam'. After independence, it advocated that Assam should secede from India and become an independent country. Really speaking separatist sentiments of the Assamese were expressed in the Language Movement (1960), Oil Refinery Movement (1976) and the Anti-Foreigner Movement (1975-1985). During the anti-foreigner movement, ULFA was formed by six college drop-outs, including Arvind Rajkhowa and Gopal Baruah. At the same time, Assam People's Liberation Army (APLA) was formed by Arpan Bezbaruah. APlA committed violent armed action by killing police officers prior to the state assembly elections in 1983.

The leaders of ULFA were the members of the All Assam Students Union (AASU) during the Assam agitation. Most of them joined the Assam Gana Parishad (AGP) government. Those who were not in the government reactivated the ULFA under the leadership of Paresh Barua. It established contact with the National Socialist Council of Nagaland (NSCN) in 1981 for procuring arms and ammunition and arranging training of its cadres.

In 1983, ULFA's activities crossed to Myanmar for training via Arunachal Pradesh and Nagaland. It reportedly has its training camps in Bhutan, Arunachal Pradesh and Nagaland, links with the Kachin Independent Army (KIA) of Myanmar, procuring arms and other material through them, reportedly from China, and contacts with the People's Liberation Army (PLA) of Manipur.[19]

ULFA fought with arms against the Government of India in order to achieve Assam's sovereignty as part of waging war. It also targetted the people from outside, mainly Bengali as a response to the question of forced assimilation. So in 1989, they started killing non-Assamese particularly those having big business in Assam, and also carried out large-scale extortions. The government has not been able to check its violent activities. It is alleged that the Judiciary has been lenient towards it and AGP government was soft on it. Military action too has been unsuccessful. Even the operation Bajrang did not eliminate any hardcore terrorist nor captured any sophisticated or many weapons. Tdays The bases of UNLF in Bangladesh and Myanmar could be used by them. It has maintained close relationship with various militant groups of Manipur also.

Some Details of Politics of Secessionism in Assam

Girin Phukan remarks that an assumption, movements of NE region being spear-headed by some foreign agents with an ulterior motive, is not the sole criterion to understand the centrifugal urges of these groups. Further, he gives his argument that while there may be some substance in it in the sense that different foreign agents may have taken advantage of the sentiments of those groups; nevertheless the activities of the foreign agents are not real sources of their separatist feeling. The ingredients of secessionist urges in this region may be traced back to the pre-independence period. Without the knowledge of legacy of these urges, the current problem of liberation movement in the northeast cannot be understood properly. He attempts to partially understand the feeling of the Assamese alone and focused categorically in his article "Politics of Secessionism in Northeast India".[20]

Surprisingly, though it may see, even the Brahmaputra valley which had a cultural link with India prior to the British occupation, today feels virtually a sense of alienation from the rest of the country. The Assamese who had been the dominant group of the valley ever since the British conquest of Assam are facing the crisis of their lingo-cultural identity as a result of continuous immigration from outside the state and feel a sense of deprivation of their 'legitimate share' in respect of economic development. This, in turn, gives a fillip to the rise of Assamese national sentiment. It may, however, be noted that regional nationalism is not always contrary to national integration in a federation like ours. But excessive emphasis on regional nationalism obviously leads to the growth of secessionism. This trend has been very much discernible in the regional movements in Assam. As a result, the anti-foreigner movement in Assam (1979-85) gave birth to an extremist organization named Untied Liberation Front of Assam (ULFA) in April, 1979 which seeks to establish an independent sovereign Assam outside the Indian Union.[21] Although the ULFA is splited and bulk of its members have surrendered, the role of their extremist organization would largely determine the trend and nature of politics of the region. It is interesting that secessionist urge of this section of the Assamese is not a new phenomenon rather it existed even prior to independence. Therefore, in order to have a better understanding of the current secessionist movement, one must be aware of its legacy.

Ever since the British occupation, there had been a continuous flow of non-Assamese into Assam. In fact, in order to run the imperialist administration, clerks and officers familiar with the system of company Administration were brought in by the British from outside the province particularly from Bengal. The Marwaris and few Biharis came to fill the necessities of trade and business created by the opportunities of economic expansion under the British rule. A certain number of other people came to fill the various demands of colonial economic development. Thus, people had come to Assam (1) from Rajasthan, U.P. etc. as businessmen, (2) from Eastern Bengal as settlers on agricultural land, clerical staff and small traders; (3) from Bihar, U.P. , Orissa and Tamil Nadu as tea garden labourers and other manual labourers; and (4) as live-stock farmers from Nepal. So rapid and the large immigration was from Bengal, C.S. Mullan, a British Census Commissioner, commented in his Census Report of 1931 that immigration was likely to alter permanently the whole future of Assam and to destroy more surely than the Burmese invasion of 1820 the whole structure of Assamese culture and civilization.[22] Thus, it appeared to the Assamese that non-Assamese people threatened the very existence of what they chose to call the "Assamese Nation". After 1925, the provincial Government of Assam was mostly dominated by the Muslim League. The Assamese elites were convinced that the Muslim League Ministry led by Muhammad Saddulla adopted a deliberate policy of encouraging East Bengal Muslims to come to Assam with the design to increase the ratio of Muslim population of Assam.[23] They further believed that this was done in order to perpetuate Muslim

League's powers in Assam if not to make Assam a part of proposed Pakistan. Besides, the Bengali Hindu immigrants in Assam alone constituted a sizeable part of the population and since the Muslim immigrants also happened to be Bengalis linguistically, they combined with the Bengali Hindus constituting larger Bengali population. The increase of Bengali population in the province appeared to be a 'threat' to the socio-cultural and even political identity of the Assamese. They had to face keen competition in their own home even for job and in the field of petty trade and business with its counterpart, the immigrant communities. The introduction of 'Bengalee' as the official language of the province in 1837 had yet another effect in this direction which enabled the Bengalees to compete with them. After the partition of the country in 1947, the streams of Bengalee refugees into Assam further reinforced this threat. Thus the Assamese elite found themselves in constant fear and anxiety of being gradually dominated by the Bengalees both culturally and politically. They even had a fear that Assam would become a part of the proposed 'Greater Bengal' if the Bengali immigrants remained unchecked. Second, Muslim immigration from Bengal began to be viewed as a calculated move to turn Assam into a Muslim majority province so that she could qualify herself for inclusion into the erstwhile East Pakistan, now Bangladesh.

Over and above, the Assamese elite were very much concerned about the economic backwardness of Assam. Despite being potentially one of the richest provinces in the Indian Union., Assam found herself economically backward. The Assamese elite called it a rich province with the poor people.[24] As a cause of backwardness the Assamese elite thought that the center was taking away too much revenue from Assam; while the Government of

Assam, on the other hand did not get its 'legitimate share' of the duties on tea, oil, jute, coal etc. In addition to this, the Assamese elite felt a sense of insecurity from the point of view of what they called, "economic exploitation" by the outsiders. As noted earlier, the modern sinews of life such as employment, trade, business, etc. were largely in the hands of the non-Assamese residents of Assam. The scope for government jobs was limited, the economic infrastructure for industrialisation was grossly inadequate and land and forest were not adequately used for the economic development of Assam. Whatever employment opportunities were available, the educated Assamese middle class elite had to face keen competition with the non-Assamese. The non-Assamese were having their earning from this area by engaging themselves in industry, trade, and commerce which they did not fully reinvest in the area as could have been done. A considerable part of it were drained to their native homes. The result was that the economic growth of this region was slowed down and fresh employment opportunities which could have forged links between the entrepreneurs from outside and the local people did not develop. The tea companies which were largely in the hands of the foreigners did not give any direct benefit to Assam. The non-Assamese middle class not only had much greater earnings, but their style of living stood in sharp contrast to that of the native people of the province; which in turn only helped to increase bitterness. The partition of the country snapped the direct transport link between Assam and the rest of the country, it made the rail and road link circuitous. This seriously affected the economic development of Assam. Low productivity in agriculture and the consequent prevalence of widespread poverty provided ideal breeding ground for the development of secessionist feelings. The Assamese elite began to think that the central government and the rest of India were not interested in the well being of Assam. There was also a lurking fear among the Assamese elite that the parliament, having larger representation from bigger states should control the economic lot of the small states like Assam and that the few representatives from Assam would have no impact on the decision of the parliament.[25]

It was very much in the minds of the Assamese elite that economically Assam yet remained a backward province in spite of her enormous economic potentialities. They were not happy with the existing financial adjustment between the center and Assam which they characterized as 'unscientific' and inequalities' and alleged that it constituted a grave injustice done to Assam.[26] Hence, they believed that her economic backwardness could be removed only if she became an independent state.

Yet another group of Assamese intellectuals articulated the idea of sovereign independent political status for Assam on the ground of Assam's socio-cultural distinctness and historical background. They asserted that the Assamese, who constituted the dominant group in Assam, formed a sufficiently distinctive group from the point of view of language and culture. They believe that the development of language and culture could be fostered, if Assam have made a separate independent state.

In addition to these, different ethnic groups such as the tribals and the Ahoms, who are the constituents at the larger Assamese society, had also expressed remarkable centrifugal sentiments separately at the advent of independences. It may be noted that the plain tribals like the Bodos who were the original inhabitants of Assam became apprehensive of the possible 'danger' from the non-Assam Indians of the province. It was very often complained that the non-Assamese cultivators particularly from Bengal, had been allowed to occupy lands within the tribal belts. In fact, the tribal elites were critical of the immigration policy of the Saadulla government which they characterized as a "policy of invitation" to landless peasants.[27] They felt that no efforts were being made either by Muslim League or by the Congress to safeguard their interest. This led them to believe that the increasing number of non-tribals in the tribal belts in particular, and non-Assamese Indians in the province, in general, were posing threat to the tribal identity while being conscious of their distinct identity and anxious to pressure and develop their own socio-cultural heritage. Some of the tribal elite thought to make their, what they called, 'homeland' (Assam) a sovereign independent state outside the Indian Union. They believe that if Assam became free, the influx of non-Assamese Indians into Assam could be checked and the tribals would be in a better position to protect their interest.

Thus the present separatist urges of a section of the Assamese are not entirely the product of post-independent period. These were rather rooted in the past. As a measure maintaining distinct Assamese identity, a section of Assamese elite expressed secessionist sentiment in the middle and the late forties, within the framework of Indian federation. They believed, the 'legitimate' Assamese interest would not be protected. Hence, they wanted to make Assam separate from the rest of the country. Even after more than five decades of independence, similar feelings and sentiments have been persisting and at present it has been able to find greater expression and articulation.

It is necessary to note that during the last decades, no attention has been paid to these feelings and sentiments of the Assamese expressed even prior to independence. As a result, separatist sentiments appear to have been articulated in different regional movements such as the Language Movements, 1960; Oil Refinery Movement, 1967; movement on the issue of Medium of Instruction, 1972; and finally the Anti-Foreigner Movement 1979-85 gave birth to a formal secessionist organization i.e. ULFA. In fact, there is nothing new in the present demands of the articulate section of the Assamese and also the demands made by the ULFA. But to day ULFA seems to be in process of peace talk.

At the beginning of 2005, Delhi University Professor Mamoni Rasain Goswami made efforts to bring ULFA to the negotiating table. In this context, an open Forum on the theme of Government of India – Ultra Negotiation was held on 22nd January 2005 at Gauhati University organised by Law Department of the Gauhati University. The forum was chaired by Professor Naorem Sanajaba, Head of the Department of Law, Gauhati University. In it Prof. G.N.Talukdar, Vice-Chancellor of Gauhati University, expressed the necessity of discussing on the issue of negotiations between the government and the ultras keeping in view the desire of the people of Assam for an early solution.

Professor Niru Hazarika, ex-Dean of Arts, Gauhati University, in her erudite deliberation on the problem of insurgency and the government initiatives welcomed the present trend towards holding effective negotiation to arrive at an acceptable and just solution. She pointed out a number of other pertinent aspects which will have to be looked into, before a solution can be mooted out. State force invites counter force from the insurgents, she said. Identification of the actual political situation is a must and this will augment the emergence of alternatives. Interpretation of law is necessary in the context of the current political situation. She opined that since the objective of the state is the welfare of the people, the talks may, be held on the question of sovereignty also. She referred to the emergence of pressure groups and said that the process of collective bargaining can be commenced only after considering the interest of the majority. Constitutional morality is to be observed not only by the mass but also by the rulers. The people are the foundation of political entity, and therefore, it is for them to decide the question of sovereignty or popular sovereignty.

Shri D. C. Mahanta , Senior Advocate, High Court dwelt on the question whether there was any provision in the Constitution for discussion on the question of sovereignty. If not, the question of discussion on it should not arise. He felt that it was more an issue relating to development of the country. He narrated an instance where he had, in an article in a newspaper, urged the ultras to return home and concentrate on development of the state, but there was no response. He exhorted that, it is the wish of the people that the ultras should return home for an honourable solution.

Mr. Nilay Dutta, Advocate General of Nagaland whilespeaking on the status of the Government of India, stated that under the Constitution, power is vested in the three organs, viz., legislature, judiciary and executive and that the state can function as only one unit of the authority so vested. The Government of India has to act within the judicial boundaries and enunciations of the Supreme Court. Matters of high state policy cannot be tried by the media and should be taken up 'in camera'.

On the aspect of the ultras, he explained that they are to be identified, in terms of their demands whether they are within the purview of the Constitution or outside the purview of the Constitution. He identified the ultra groups of J&K and those of Punjab (since contained) as being outside the purview of the constitution, while PWG of Bihar was within the purview of the constitution. In the North-East, the NSCN and the ULFA are outside the purview, while the BLT, the DHD, the Hmar Liberation Army and the DMD are within the purview. He wondered why the latter, demanding only statehood or a district council, should choose to take up arms. Obviously, the same solution cannot be imposed on all the ultra groups. There is a lack of knowledge of the central authority regarding the delineations. Speaking on the authority to negotiate, he clarified that Art. 253 provides for the power of the government to conclude a treaty with any other country and enter into international agreements. If the GOI. is to make any agreement with such party, it will have to invite third party intervention. To that extent, the ultra's demand for talks through a third party is legitimate. In such cases, international conventions may be opted for. Examples are East Timor and the USA-Vietcong conflicts. On the matter of the power of secession, he referred to the Re Birubari case, wherein the decision of the Supreme Court was to transfer an area of land to Bangladesh, which however, could not be fully implemented, as the constitutionality of the transfer was challenged. Further, he mentioned that as per Art. 368, the amendment of the Constitution required a two-third majority, which is not always available. Mr.Dutta also referred to the Keshavananda Bharati case, where it was decided that, the 'basic structure' of the Constitution could not be changed. Any negotiation, must take into consideration all the facts mentioned. Ultimately, the advisory opinion of the Supreme Court may be obtained, before any negotiation is initiated. He added that the Hindi/cow belt neglected nationality questions of the N E region in 1947.

Prof. Srinath Barua, ex-Dean, Faculty of Arts, Gauhati university, while stating that the question of finding a solution is very complex, lamented that there were internal and external forces which were engaged in procrastinating on the matter of a solution. Further, there was lack of in-depth knowledge regarding the actual objectives of the ultras. He asserted that negotiation can also take place outside the country. At the same time, the views of the people should also be taken into account, without which no solution will be acceptable to the majority. Finally, he opined that as there was no provision in the Constitution for discussion on sovereignty, the question for according greater powers may be discussed.. He also cited the role of espionage agencies used by the countries.

Shri H.N. Das, Former Chief Secretary, Government of Assam, while attempting to bring out the historical perspective and genesis of the issue of insurgency in the state, recalled that the first movement in the state, was launched by Arpan Bezbaruah of Tezpur on the basis of ethnicity. On the subject of ethnicity, he went back to the days of 'Sukapha', whose advent heralded the creation of the composite Assamese society. He went through the Burmese invasion and the Treaty of Yandaboo and then to the attempt of the British to remove the Assamese language from it's use in the Courts. He lauded the contributions of the American missionaries to the consolidation of the Assamese language. Shri Das spoke of his research work done in 1983-84, wherein he had made the following observations:

(1) Assam was better off in 1953 than in 1983.

(2) Assam was always granted funds by the Centre, less than what the Planning Commission envisaged for the state.

(3) The growth rate in Assam at present, is far less than that of the earlier period.

He emphasized that economic hardship is a primary factor for the popular discontent. He had two prescriptions for the negotiation process-.(a) Rigid legalities are to be avoided, (2) Negotiations should be done in camera and persons with logic and not influenced by emotion, should be involved in the talks. In respect of administrative efficiency, which is also a factor, he pointed out the growth and development of Tripura, which he attribute to the keeping down of corruption to the minimum and administrative efficacy. He has also observed that insurgency and development are both compatible in Tripura.

Several questions have been raised during interaction. On the conclusion of the speaker's session, the chairman of the open forum, Professor Naorem Sanajaoba, Head of the Department of Law, Gauhati University, presented a resume of the address delivered by the main speakers, in the open debate on GOI- Insurgency (ULTRA) political negotiation. He has also added the practices and mechanisms for talks.

He recalled the negotiation within the frame work of the Constitution, as deliberated upon by the other speakers. Besides, he also briefly mentioned the tested standard of political negotiations followed in similar situations, by way of describing the test cases of :- (1) Vietnam, (2) Palestine Issue, (3) Great Britain-Irish Republican Army, political negotiations in 1998,(4) the on going Srilanka-Tamil Eelam insurgency and (5) the conduct of international relations, as in the case of Eastern Timor, now known as Timor Liste. These standard political negotiations are invariably conducted, with the necessary presence of a third party, International Guarantor (preferably a superpower, or the U.N.) Acceptance of the Framework of Negotiations and Principle of Negotiation, between the parties involved, (as in the case of the IRA Negotiations 1998), or International Facilitator, (as in the case of Tamil Eelam), is indispensable for successful and actually result oriented talks.These boundary conditions and parameters, are the necessary requirements of a successful negotiation between the parties concerned, in similar situations. As regards the GOI-NSCN negotiations during the last eight years, no comment could be given, as none of the standard procedures had been followed and no framework or principle of negotiation had been laid down by the parties concerned, and above all, the negotiation was conducted by a domestic interlocutor, that is, by one of the two parties in conflict. However, Prof. Naorem Sanajaoba briefly stated that, better and more effective form of negotiation, süi generis, could also be evolved, in addition to the tested and the standard procedures of negotiation. A framework, structure and principles, are the basic and elementary requirements for delivering results, tangible and material.

Meghalaya

Like other people of NE, the Khasis of Meghalaya have a tendency to separate from India and want to remain as sovereign state in the history of Meghalaya during the time of merger to India in 1947. During this period, the leaders of Khasi signed the standstill agreement with India, and later decided not to join the Union. Sib Syiem, a Khasi leader, was persuaded to sign the instrument of Accession with India, which was opposed by his nephew, Wickliffe Syiem, who at that time was in Sylhet to sign a treaty of friendship with Pakistan. He submitted an appeal to the United Nations (UN) in March 1942, protesting against the merger with India. But the tendency of Khasi people could not put into practice. They remained silent more than two decades. They were only at stake when the Assam government decided to introduce the Assamese as the official language in the state. So the All-Party Hill Leaders' Conference (APHLC) was formed to lead a movement for the separate hill state. The result was that the Khasi people secured an autonomous region of Meghalaya in 1970 and got full-fledged state in 1972.

The rise of insurgency in Meghalaya was visualized in 1989 with the formation of Meghalaya United Movement(MUM). Its main objectives was all round development of the Khasi society and in due course of secession from Indian union, when the idea became acceptable to the society at large. A few volunteers joined MUM. The group had some small arms. The MUM had a working arrangement with the ULFA. regarding their passage to and from Bangladesh.

In 1991, Achik Liberation Matgrik Army (ALMA) came into being with the main objective of creating a separate Garo-land, comprising of the inhabited areas of Meghalaya, Assam and Bangladesh. Other objectives of ALMA included eradication of corruption and action against foreign nationals. The ALMA also had working relationship with the ULFA and the NSCN.

In 1992, another insurgent group came into existence, namely the Hynniewtrip Voluntary Council (HVC). The main objective of the council was eradication of social evils which affect the Khasi society especially the youth. The council had working arrangement with the ULFA for passage from and to Bangladesh as in the case of Meghalaya United Movement (MUM).

In the year 1992 itself, Hynniewtrip Achik Liberation Council (HALC) was formed to promote secessionist ideology amongst the youth. It has a 21-point charter of demand. The council focuses on armed revolution for complete separation from the Indian Union. The council has a working arrangement with the NSCN.

According to S.K. Agnihotri, there are four phases of their movement. In the first phase, a core group is formed accompanied by low-level propaganda. There is a limited recruitment of volunteers and the incidents are isolated. In this phase, administrative response is minimal. The phase is considered as a police problem and limited operation were undertaken. The second phase is the build-up phase when memorandum picks up. The insurgent group increases the recruitment of volunteers and undertakes additional propaganda measures. The frequency of incidents also increases and weaponry is also procured. In the third phase it is quit stand still though there is mushrooming of insurgents. As a result, cracks develop in the solidarity of various sub-groups, and at the same time the administrative response also becomes more professional and operations ete., in comparison and more successful. The last phase of insurgency is the declining phase. Their enthusiasm gets diminished. The number of incidents go down and some groups want to come over ground.

At present two insurgent groups, Hynniewtrep Achik Liberation Council (HALC) and Achik National Volunteer Council (ANVC) are active. though the insurgent groups of Meghalaya are not posing a serious threat to internal security, they are capable of systematic extortions including from government servants.[28]

Mizoram

Mizoram was also hot bed of armed struggle before 1980 when Mizo National Front was so strong. They revolted in the sixties against the authority of the Indian Union demanding with self-determination with external only that means creation of a new state within the country. In the mid 1980s, the government signed-the Mizo accord to end the 20 years insurgency problem in Mizoram . Mizoram has since been benefited with significant funds from the centre as part of a 'development package'. A section of the militants of the erstwhile underground mizo national front are, however, unhappy. Their complaint is the funds meant for the resettlement of the former rebels have been misappropriated. Under the banner of Peace Accord Mizo National Front Returnees Association (PAMRA), a memorandum was submitted to Chief Minister, these former rebels threatened to launch a peaceful agitation for getting their demand was not conceded. Meanwhile, 13 insurgency – related incidents occurred in the border areas of Mizoram since December 1998 where militants of the neighboring states and those based in Myanmar and Bangladesh had taken refugee. Five policemen lost their lives while fighting the insurgents and one policeman was kicked by an irate mob during the period.

Arunachal Pradesh

Arunachal Pradesh, erstwhile NEFA ,in comparison with other states of NE, is one of the most peaceful and free from insurgency movement state. But it becomes base areas of NSCN and ULFA Still they are operating like their homelands.

Tribal rebels of the NSCN are reportedly terrorizing businessmen for ransom in the eastern districts of Tirap and Changlang, bordering Myanmar, and threatening politicians to endorse their demand for a federally administered territory to be carved out of the area. The ULFA militants are setting up bases in the state because of having hesitation to be uncordial relationship with Bhutanese troops after persuasion made by Government of India.

From the details given above,about the militant groups of NE India, one comes to understand that the sensitive insurgency prone states of NE are Assam, Manipur and Tripura only as there exist armed struggle in their state. But the notable thing is that they have more or less the same problems and discontentment. They seemed to be ailed by the existing political system. So prediction can be made that all the states supposed to fight against the Union Government together if the Government doesn't try to resolve the conflict and to see what their discontentment and political aspirations are.

Here one of the most important areas to draw attention and need to study is the political aspiration of the armed opposition groups of the people. According to them their resistance is the class struggle in between the oppressed people and oppressor. They are oppressed in the sense that their territory was occupied by the foreign oppressor after snatching the sovereignty of their nation. Now their nation is under the control of occupying force with imposition of many black laws including AFSPA 1958. All their rights seem to be under the military booths. They have also stated that this is not waging war against the Indian government by them. This is war against war. They have launched active resistances against the hidden war done by foreign oppressor. By their hidden war, it may mean the snatching of sovereignty, operating by occupying forces and violation of human rights is being done. They have also given clarification that theirs is not a separatist movement, they simply appeal that the Government of India and its security forces should leave from their occupying land.[29] They have firm determination and still going on to fight against Indian security forces. They also defy the peace talk proposed by both the state and central government.

Further, they also give clarification that they could not be branded as terrorists on the ground that their organisation is in the position of signatory of common Article 3 of Geneva Convention.[30] And no one should use even the term insurgency against them because their National Liberation Movement against an existing political system (Government) is supported by the people either to have revolutionary government or party is justified.

NOTES AND REFERENCES

1. Girin Phukan, Politics of Secessionism in Northeast India, in eds.,B.Pakem, *Insurgency in North-East India*, New Delhi, 1997, p.255.
2. R.S. Jassal has given the names of various outfits of the Northeastern states and their area of operation.According to him- Revolutionary People's Front (RPF) and its armed wing People's Liberation Army (PLA), United National Liberation Front (UNLF) & its armed wing (Manipur Peoples' Army) (MPA), People's Revolutionary Party of Kangleipak (PREPAK) & its armed wing Red army,

Kangleipak Communist Party (KCP), Kanglei Yawol Kanna Lup(KYKL), United Kuki Liberation Front(UKLF), Kuki National Army(KNA), Kuki National Front(KNF), Zoumi Revolutionary Army (ZRA), Hmar People's Convension (HPC), Hmar Revolutionary Front (HRF), National Socialist Council of Nagaland-Issac/Muivah [NSCN(IM)],National Socialist Council of Nagaland-Khaplang [NSCN(K)], Naga National Council-Khadao [NNC(K)], Naga National Council-(Adino) [NNC(A)], EKRF-EKLA, North Eastern Minority Front (NEMF), Kuki Defence Force(KDF), Kuki Revolutionary Army(KRA), Kuki Liberation Army (KLA). The organisations operating in Nagaland are- NSCN(IM), NSCN(K), NNC(A), KYKL (Operating areas of Nagaland, Dimapur, Gharpani along NH-39), KNF(Kuki dominated areas of Dimapur and NE Hills) are thehe outfits operating in Manipur. In Assam, the organisations active in the state are United Liberation Front of Asom (ULFA), National Democratic Front of Bodoland(NDFB), United Peoples' Democratic Solidarity (UPDS) KLO, Boro Liberation Tiger(BLT), Dima Haolim Doaga(DHD), Karbi National Volunteer(KNV), RNSF, KRLOKPF, TNRF, BEF, BTF, AEF, ASF, AAASS, GTF, BVYLF,MULTA, MSCA, MSCA, ULMA, ILAA, MVF, MLA, MSF, ISS, IURPI, UMLFA, RMC, MTF, PULF, AS, HARKUL MUJAHIDEEN. In Arunachal Pradesh too, there are outfits active in the state. They are- Liberation Tigers of Arunachal (LTA), National Liberation Army(NLA), United Liberation Tigers (ULT) Revolutionary Army of Aruncahal(RAA) NSCN(IM) in Tirap, NSCN(K). In Tripura also there are outfits operating in the state. They are - National Liberation Front of Tripura(NLFT), and All Tripura Tribal Force (ATTF). In Mizoram, the outfits operating in the state are Bru National Liberation Force(BNLF), Arakans Liberation Party(ALP). In Meghalaya too, there are outfits operating in the state. They are Heyiewtrap National Liberation Council (HNLC),Achik National Voluntary Council (ANVC), Khasi Students Organisation (KSO) cited in Comdt. RS Jassal (Retd), *Manipur: Insurgency Redefined,* paper presented in the Seminar

3. Donn Morgan Kipgen: Unity in diversity, *The Sangai Express*, 5 February, 2005, Imphal.
4. R.K. Jhaljit Singh, *A Short History of Manipur*, Imphal, 1965, p.34.
5. L. Ibungohal Singh, *Introduction to Manipur*, Imphal, 198,p.165
6. Naorem Sanajaoba, *Manipur: Past and Present*, vol. 1, Mittal Publications, New Delhi, 1998, p.254.
7. *ibid.*
8. *ibid.*, p.255
9. *Manipur State Constitution Act, 1947* (Art 3 of the chapter 1).
10. Naorem Sanajaoba, The Genesis of Insurgency, in eds., Naorem Sanajaoba, *Manipur: Past and Present*, vol.1, Delhi, 1988, p.256.
11. Mahraja's *letter* to an official of Government of India, named Prakash, *Resistance*, 2 October 1979.
12. *Resistance, 25* September 1979.
13. Phanjoubam Tarapot, *Insrugency Movement in North East India*, Har Anand Publications, New Delhi, 1994, p.63
14. Press note released by Ad-hoc Committee Royal Labour Reserve Task Front- *Maning Tambasingbu Singnaba*, 6.6.1985, p.l
15. Irengbam Chaoren, *Eina Yaon Lambisigi Khongun Libada*, tr., *When I trace the Genesis of the Revolution*, dt. and place of publication not cited, p.4. The author is the Chairman of the proscribed Revolutionary peoples' Front (RPF) whose armed wing is Peoples Liberation Army (PLA).
16. *n 13.*
17. *The Sangai Express*, 3 February 2005.
18. Bhattachatryya, S, *Genesis of Tribal Extremism in Tripura*, New Delhi, Gyan Publishing House,1991, pp.1-2.
19. Sanjoy Hazarika, Insurgency in North East India, in eds., B.Pakem, *Insurgency in North East India*, New Delhi, 1997. p.119

20. Girin Phukan, *op.cit.*, p.256.
21. *Ibid.*, p.257.
22. *Census Report of India (Assam)*, 1931, Vol.III, Part. 1, p.49.
23. Harendranath Baruah, The Development Scheme, Position of Indigenous People, in *The Assam Tribune*, August 29, 1949.
24. Sabhapati Abhivashan, Arthanitik Aru Samajik Sakha (in Assamese), *Seventeenth Session Asom Sahitya Sabha proceedings*, Guwahati, 1937.
25. *n 20.*, p.260.
26. *The Assam Tribune,* 24 December 1949.
27. Bhimbar Deroi's Speech, *Assam Legislative Council Proceedings,* Vol. 1, 26 February 1940, p.103.
28. S.K. Agnihotri, Background Note on Militancy in Meghalaya, in eds., B. Pakem, *Insurgency in North East India,* Delhi, 1997, p.313.
29. Memorandum submitted by RPF to the Chairman, Decolonisation Committee (Committee of 24) United Nations Geneva/ New York Headquarters on 11 December 1996, p.xv.
30. RPF and its Army Wing PLA became signatory of Common Article 3 of Geneva Convention in 1997.

4

COUNTER INSURGENCY OPERATIONS

The Government of India's policies towards the NE is much identical to the policy framed and implemented in India by the British during the colonial regime. As British policies towards North East, every possible attempt was made to isolate the tribals from the rest of the country. For instance, restriction of the present political system in which political visions of tribal areas of Nagaland, Mizoram and Arunachal - Pradesh are restricted is the hangover from the British period.

Even long after the British deliberately kept these tribal areas isolated, it is unfortunate that the Indian Government, after independence, had paid little sympathy to the deep rooted problems of this area for several years. It failed to solve the vexed problems of lack of means of communications in these difficult terrain which posed a serious problem of communication and development of local societies was basically left to the care of the missionaries. It was only in 1962-63, after the Chinese had begun to mount their attack from this NE border, the Indian Government had realized the vulnerability of the Himalayan borders to foreign attacks and thus attempts were to be made for the development of this region.

By this time, already much damage had been done to the psyche of the local population who had little sympathy for the Indian Government which had willfully neglected this area and hardly tried to assuage the feelings and aspirations of the local population. No surprise, the leading tribals like the Nagas and the Mizos, who were also under the maximum influence of Christianity, were not able to see eye to eye with the Indian Government; rather they nursed the feeling of hostility and often had dreams of independence – a movement which had been strengthened after the Chinese attack when racially as well as geographically they found themselves more close to China than India. Further China had helped the local dissident forces in the NE with resources and arms as well trained them in Guerrilla warfare which were the most suitable to insurgencies in view of the dense jungles of these region.

Another attitude of the ruling elites of the Central Government towards the people of NE states, when they were confronted by any problems is really negative It could be cited here the worst famines faced by the Mizos in 1950's. It is well known that during the late 1950s the Mizos' district (Mizoram came later) had to face one of the worse famines when all of a sudden the emergence of a large number of rates destroyed food, crops, and forests. It posed a virtual picture of destruction and complete helplessness. The situation was further complicated due to lack of communication facilities which stood in the way of rushing help at this crucial juncture.

It is obvious that on such occasion those who have

stocks of food grains would try to capitalize on the helplessness of the local population. Since most of the traders were from the non-Mizo areas, such anti-social behaviour on their part should have aggravated the situation. It consequently led to resentment by the local population. Besides, the Government machinery, as usual, was quite tardy in rushing help which only provoked further resentment and thus strengthened the feeling of alienation from India.

While discussing about insurgencies, one cannot overlook the fact that such a colossal degree of distress following the famine, had encouraged the dissident force to come to the force and take the advantage of the situation by attracting the maximum possible local sympathy and this turning, though initially innocuous situation into a major insurgency.

The Government of India would not give full confidence to the people of NE regarding the protection of them as was happening in Sino-Indian war in 1962. In that war, Nehru, the then Prime Minister of India in his speech broadcasted in the radio stated that he could not protect the people of NE; so they could protect themselves and determine their future.In it he gave departing addresses to the people of the region. Till date, the people of Assam and other NE states very often mention it as a perfect example of neglecting the NE.

Assertion of National Interest and Reaction of this Region

The British, for their own colonial interest, introduced industrial economy with its money market, accompanied by the extension of Railway, Post and Telegraph and a wide network of communication system and spread of colonial education etc. brought together all parts of India in highly centralized administration and a common national feeling was gradually roused as against the colonial rule. In such a way Indian nationalism grew as by-product of bourgeois development which however did not grow by abolishing feudal elements and pre-feudal primitive tribal system. In this sense, there was no such industrial revolution in India like the one occured in the Western world. Whatever industrial development was there, it was of an uneven character and some areas as in the NE region remained backward in all respects. So the spirit of Indian nationalism did not spread in this region simultaneously as it did in the developed areas of the country. However, though late, capitalized money market gradually penetrated the areas of Northeastern region also, displacing nationalism based on distinctive languages, cultures etc of different groups of people. As we know along with "Bande Mataram", "Bang Emir Janani Amar", "O Mor Aponar Desh" were also sung as national songs in Bengal and Assam during the national movement.[1] We may consider in the same spirit the gradual emergence of the Nagas, the Mizos and others from their respective ethnic to a nascent national or sub-national status. As a matter of fact, the Nagas, who were the first to initiate their movements in 1946, demanded their autonomy within Assam and Mizos followed suit. In Manipur also, in its contemporary times, Irawat's movement with arms were started and it is still continued by various underground organizations .[2]

To counter the threat from the forces of separatism the ruling class in the country are trying their level best to accomplish the triple objectives of the region planning, i.e. economic development, sovereignty and national integration. In the age of globalisation we are told that we need to achieve national integration within and integration of India in the world market for proper development. It is irony that India that had its origin in the historic struggle against the world imperialism in the 19th and the 20th centuries is today actively propagating the ideology of neo-imperialism. The forces of globalisation that are being unleashed in the form of the World Trade Organisations (WTO) have opened the process of neo-colonialism the world over and the people are its worst victims.

But most of the insurgent groups incorporated the term National in moving their organisation (The Naga National Council). The Newsletter published by them was named "The Naga Nation"; Mizos also had their "Mizo National Front". Besides, many of the insurgent groups mentioned the term liberation in their nomenclature ULFA, PLA which gave a fillip to other insurgent groups to emerge. All these illustrate the feeling of nationalism and urge for liberating their respective peoples from the different insurgent groups of the NE region. Even Assam which is comparatively more developed and more closely interlinked with the mainland is no exception, as the region has been experiencing armed struggle with the proclaimed objective of fighting for the liberation of Assamese from colonial yoke of Indian Union.

The question is not to correlate Indian nationalism with regional sub-nationalism as has emerged in the different part of the NE region. If we stuck to the pre-conceived idea of India being a nation-state the constrictions would seem to be insurmountable. But if we accepted the fact of India, being a multinational state, comprising different racial, linguistic, cultural groups of people, aspiring for enjoying equal share of power, democratic rights etc. within the federal structure of Indian state, the assumed contradiction would vanish. As we know, many of the developed states have been clamoring for wider autonomy for their states, while firmly standing for '*Indian unity and integrity*' implying unity for all pervasive capitalist market and any demand for demanding or strengthening regional autonomy is deemed anti-national.

Specific Features of India

The world today can be broadly divided into three types of countries: (a) independent monopoly capitalist countries, (b) colonial and semi-feudal countries (c) semi-colonial and semi feudal countries. India is neither an independent country like USA, UK, France etc. nor a colony of a particular imperialist country as it was before 1947. It is a semi-colonial country of the neo-colonial type in its external relation, while in its internal relation it is neither a capitalist country nor a completely feudal country. Rather it can be called a semi-feudal because feudalism is still predominant here in the overall production system. This specific feature of colonialism in India distinguishes it from many other countries of the world in the present epoch.[3]

Counter Insurgency Operations

The people of NE India have witnessed three major military operations as part of counter insurgency operations. They are Operation Bazrang, Operation Rhino and Operation Blue Bird. Though this counter insurgency could stop the insurgents 'outfits' activities with much effectiveness, it only remains in the minds of the people and ask themselves whether they are citizens of India or not. The question can be answered by the following summaries of military operation in Assam, Nagaland and Manipur.

Human Rights Violation in Assam(Operations Rhino 1991)

Operation rhino was first started on the night of 14th September 1991. On that night, about 40-50 thousand Jawans of the Indian Army belonging to Crack Mountain Divisions, Kumaon Regiment, Rajputna Rifles and other units under the command of 4 Crore HQ, Eastern command went into action. This force was aided by about a lakh paramilitary force personnel belonging to CRPF, BSF, Assam Rifles and the states police.

From 14th September till the time of writing this report, Assam has been virtually under military rule. The Armed Forces are operating under the provisions of the two acts namely – the Assam Disturbed Area Act, 1995 and the Armed Forces Special Power Act, 1958 (as amended in 1972).

The aforementioned Acts envisage the role of armed forces strictly as that of aiding civil administration if necessary in disturbed or dangerous conditions. The act has very clearly limited the role of the armed forces to that of providing necessary aid and not to that of usurping of the powers and the function of the administration.

But in practice, the civil administration is virtually sidetracked and marginalized. In the district level, the Deputy Commissioner and the Superintendent of Police was totally kept in the dark. The Army Co-ordination Committees that were set up to co-ordinate the actions were virtually non functional. The armed forces instead of aiding civil authorities had taken over the power and functions of civil administrations and were running the whole show. They were conducting mass raids, arrests without informing civil authorities and their operations were usually not accompanied by Magistrates as necessary under the prescribed law. At the village level, they were not even taking the *Gaonburrahs* (village headmen) with them. Not to speak of army aiding civil administrations, there was no army civilian co-ordination in the actual field of operations. In this situation, the onuses of all acts of commissions and omissions had to rest squarely on the armed forces.

As a result of such a situation:

1. Wanton army search operations, raids, mass atrocities had become common place.
2. Even the houses of sitting members of Parliament were not spared from wanton raids. The residence of Shri Nagen Saikia, Rajya Sabha member was ransacked by an army contingent in Dibrugarh. The incident was condemned in the Parliament and it came up before the privilege committee.
3. In the month of November, the army raided the house of the Judicial Magistrate without proper warrants. At first the administration tried to hush up the matter, but when the press brought out the details, including the Government memos, the Government tried to downplay the incident by declaring that an amicable settlement had been reached after the concerned army officers expressed their regret.
4. Police officers, constables, their families including their members of armed forces on leave were not spared from raids, humiliations, tortures and even murders.

5. The Army were conducting independent interrogations and tortures. These are not empowered by the laws of the land. Even after handing over a prisoner to police custody, they were forcing the police to hand over the person again to the army who was then brought to army camps, interrogated and tortured.

In short, all kinds of human rights violation like beating, hanging, wet submarine treatment, continuously pouring water, staking, frame treatment, giving electric shock were done by the army. Even deaths during Rhino operations were reported.[4]

Suicide During Army Operations

During army operations cases of deaths occurred when the persons cornered by army had no alternatives then committing suicides. There were five such known cases:[5]

1. Ajit Medhi Borbil, Digboi, on 25 October1991
2. Abhijit Kr.Phukan Borbil, Sibsagar, on 26 October 1991
3. Manoranjan Haloi Belsor, Nalbari, on 05 Novemmber 1991
4. Ranjit Bragohain Golaghat, on 03 November 1991

Army Operations in Manipur

There have been persistent and widespread reports of violations of human rights in the plains and the hills of Manipur since 1950s, when the security forces were first sent into Nagaland and Manipur. Mention should be made of some cases of the most well known abuses. In some of them, the courts had held the Government responsible for human rights abuse and eventually, faced to grant compensations to the families of the victims.

As it is widely known that whenever there is an attack on the security forces and police by the insurgents, a combing operation is conducted forthwith in the adjoining areas. This eventually disturbs the normal life and instills fears psychosis in the mind of the villagers and common people. Women, girls and children took shelter in other parts of Manipur by fleeing away from areas under combing operation, leaving their valuable properties behind because of the fear of widespread and wanton army atrocities, torture, rape, humiliation, illegal extortion and extra judicial execution etc. as the security forces run berserk among the people. This becomes a normal routine in Manipur. Such unruly situation may also break out at any time of the day on mere suspicion.[6]

Manipur valley was declared a disturbed area on 9th September 1979 and army was deployed in the valley. The Armed Forces (Assam and Manipur) Special Power Act, 1958, was extended to the whole of Manipur state which, inter alia, gave the armed forces sweeping powers to conduct search operation to ruthlessly destroy the elements of insurgency. Regarding human right violation in Manipur Shri N. Bisheswar, the then leader of PLA, stated in his book "The expression on my death bed" that "They say (Army officers) that they are here in Manipur to protect the lives of our people from the activities of the so-called extremists. But they never stop themselves from molesting our mothers and sisters, from brutally killing and torturing of the innocent people in the name of conducting counter-insurgency operation". Further he added that "considering the fact that the then PREPAK and PLA are not as strong as the Naxalites in Bengal, Bihar and U.P. and that compared to the Naxalites, the then PREPAK and PLA are not half an insurgent or revolutionaries, I see no reason why the Government open the Manipur Sector which empowers the Army with the Special Power Act, whereas the same Government did not open any Bengal Sector or Bihar Sector or U.P. Sector, even though the then revolutionaries there (the Naxalites) were hundred times bigger and stronger than those of Manipur valley in 1980. West Bengal is a border state like Manipur and also as sensitive as Manipur. But there was no Bengal Sector (the Armed Forces Special Power Act) even if the then Naxalite activities were on the Peak and hundred times bigger than those of the PREPAK and the PLA of 1980".

Taking the above fact into account, it is concluded that the opening of the Manipur Sector in 1980 is indeed politically motivated. But technically, it amounts to the invasion of the innocent people of Manipur, the PREPAK and the PLA and other organisations being used as an excuse for the undeclared war, he futrher stated.

The imposition of these particular Black Laws was against the wishes of the common people of the region. This is amply evident from the opinions expressed in media and in the form of vehement protests made by the people especially by the womens' organizations. A few excerpt, recorded below described the situation:

> "This law is a means to suppress people's rights, as and insurgency is a political problem, it needs political solution. ... to suppress the democratic rights of the people of Manipur in the name of maintaining law and order, and to scare the mass... army operation to using a sledge-hummer to kill a fly." [7]

The present writer presents a summary of some of the major events on the basis of public documents (1974-1992 early part):

1. March 4, 1974-95: Bn. BSF carried out a combing operation at Ngaprum village in the Ukhrul district of Manipur, in an attempt to flush out Naga insurgency.
2. November 11, 1978: Army operation at Kameng, abut 12 km. west from Imphal city to flush out Meetei insurgents.
3. September 7, 1979: Army deployed in the valley of Manipur under the 'Armed Forces (Assam and Manipur) Special Power Act, 1958.
4. April 26, 1980: Combing operation, conducted by CRPF at Patsoi 8 km. North-West from Imphal.
5. September 9, 1980: Combing operation by the army under disturbed areas law at Singjamei, 6 km from Imphal city.
6. July 8, 1981: Combing operation conducted by 4th Bn. Assam Rifles at Huining village in the Ukhrul district of Manipur.
7. Feb. 19, 1982 Combing operation conducted by 21st Sikh Regiment at Ukhrul.
8. March 14, 1984: Mass killing and army operation at Heirangoi Thong, 6 km. from Imphal city.
9. July 9, 1987: Combing operation by Assam Rifles at Oinam in Senapati district of Manipur.
10. March 14, 1992: Combing operation at Mongsangei about 6 km. from Imphal.

In these combing operations andcounter insurgency measures conducted by the security forces many major events of human rights violations were happened out. It can be mentioned that during such operations– rape, disappearance while in army custody, indiscriminate firing on innocent masses, third degree torture, illegal detention even including lawyers and editors of newspaper are a common occurence. Forced labour, looting and destruction of private properties were also often occured cases.

The same combing operation is being conducted by the security forces uptil now but it is slightly changed because of the people's reaction and the movement of human rights activists. But many acts of human rights violation are still going on a large scale. The Imphal based 'Civil Liberties and Human Rights Organisation (CLAHRO)' in Manipur has been working for the last one decade to restore democracy and the 'Rule of Law', where the life and security of the citizens of this region have to be guaranteed. It ha also taken the leading part in assisting the common people for taking legal actions in cases of death and disappearance while in army custody. Not only has it challenged the imposition of the 'Armed Forces Special Power Act, 1958, but also insisted on the Central Government to introduce a Mandatory provision of law for issuing "Arrest Memo" in respect of persons arrested by police and other security forces.[8] Human rights violation like disappearance, extra judicial killing, illegal detention/harassment, rape, sodomy, torture since 1980 to July 12,2004 could be seen in a report compiled by COHR (Committee on Human Rights). The said report was incorporated as an appendix of the memorandum submitted to the Hon'ble Prime Minister of India as part of the ongoing movement launched by the Apunba Lup against AFSPA .[9]

Army Operations in Nagaland

The Naga People's Movement for Human Rights (NPMHR) has been working for the last two decades to protect the fundamental rights and fundamental freedoms of the Naga people. According to them, various forms of tortures perpetrated by the armed forces (as described by the villagers) were (a) Execution in public, (b) Mass raping, (c) Deforming sex organ, (d) Mutilating limbs and body, (c) Electric shock, (f) Puncturing eyes, (g) Hanging people upside down, (h) Putting people in smoke filled room, (i) Burning down of villages, granaries and crops (j) Concentration camps and (i) Forced starvation and labour, etc.

On November 16, 1990, the NPMHR took up some case of the violations of human rights with His Excellency, the Governor of Nagaland through a representation, which was submitted by about 10,000 (ten thousand) students and villagers in a public rally-cum-peaceful procession to the Raj Bhavan and enlightened him. The extract copy is given below:

1. On March 25, 1990, Captain Hooda of Assam Rifles shot at and fatally wounded Mr. Nungshi Ao, an employee of the Nagaland Government of Zubra, hardly 20 km. from Kohima.
2. Mrs. Gono, an old woman of about 70 years was tortured and raped by a jawan of the Assam Rifles on July 19, 1990, at Zubra.
3. Following an encounter at Yankhumou Village, the armed forces went on a mad rampage. They tortured villagers, ransacked house and looted valuables. A school teacher and student were pulled out of church service and beaten. Against Supreme Court directions and restorations, the armed forces also used educational institution as concentration camps. The Neighbouring villages had a nightmares time.

4. Between October 1-5, 1990, innocent villagers of Pherima, Zuyekhu. Phiphema, Ciepama and surrounding areas experienced untold harassments and indignities. Travelers between Kohima and Dimapur on National Highway 39 were subjected to harassment likewise.

5. Between October, 12-15, 1990 most of the Northern Angami areas, comprising of 8-10 villages were subjected to various degree of torture. Entire villagers were herded into concentration camps. A Church building was again used as a concentration camp against Supreme Court directives. Women were herded like cattle; while the men were systematically tortured Chili powder was put into their eyes, while water was poured down their nostrils. Over 50 innocent villagers sustained serious injuries. The area MLA was told to shut up, when he tried to intervene. High government officials including the Home Secretary were harassed and humiliated. The officials of the Minister of Power was shot at, his body-guard disarmed at gun point and the minister had to stand with his hands up for about three hours.

Thus large scale human rights violation by security forces was being committed to all the states of NE India because of having an armed struggle in these states. So these Military operations were proving to be a key factor towards bringing a sense of alienation amongst the North eastern people from the mainland. Many cases have proved that the army did not differentiate the people and the armed insurgents. According to law, even these armed insurgents could not be punished by security forces without the decisions of courts. Examples may be given in the case of Prime Minister Indira

Gandhi's assassination. All the culprits were punished only after having decision given by the courts.

Examining Legislative Instruments forCounter-Insurgency with Special Focus on AFSPA

It is the logic that deconstruction itself is the outcome of contradiction between the centre and the marginalized periphery. In the process of deconstruction it always breaches the existing logic by means of another logic. In other words, it is really inherent contradiction. It basically has the faces of both negation and destruction. The same thing could be happened when we discuss the cause and effect relationship. The effect becomes the causes again. When you sit on the thorn, you will get pain then and try to find out how you get pain. That is the thorn. If you are not getting pain, you will not try to search the thorn. Like that if the AFSPA (Armed Forces Special Power Act) does not cause death and torture to the innocent people, why should we cry for repealing of such act from the region. In short, the extra-judicial executions of innocent civilian populace and other forms of naked human rights violation remain a fact of life in NE states of India for the last four decades. This is the unanswered question. Central Government has given more power to the security personnel. In short, the people of the region is now in the dead end and will continue to do so if the act is not repealed.

As far as examining legislative instruments for counter liberation army (insurgency) is concerned, we need to see the cause and the effect of the issue. It is not law and order problem and it should not be conceived that it is due to unemployment and misleading of all. It is the distorted perception in the form of official projections. In reality, it is the contradiction between re-colonisation and decolonisation by having deep organizational class structure of the oppressed people. As a consequence there is class struggle in between the oppressed and the oppressor. It is being sustained by historical legacy and its importance. Historical evidences are that (i) Manipur and Tripura had been annexed to the Indian political fold, after two years of Indian independence; (ii) Assam became a part of British India not by her choice but by the choice of Burma and the British, who signed the Treaty of Yandaboo in 1826; (iii) the ethnic tribes who remained in the excluded hill areas of Assam fused themselves in the last five decades into nationhood and claimed independence prior to the passage of Indian Independence Act 1947, and the British also created India as a totally different entity from the original Indian nation that continued for centuries in the Gangatic basin. The British-created India has been a deliberate political creation, unlike the homogenous Indian nation, based on Aryabrata. The issue is, therefore, no secession, but it is about fixing the region to India by hammer and Tongs.[10]

Prof. Sanajaoba Naoriya analysed it from the political angle and stated as "the creation of nascent entity which has passed through diverse – and even, non-complementary historical experiences. The sub-terranean fault lines are cracking up and the Indian state persists in quick fixing the deep-structured faultiness with the help of the powerful Indian army and state repression, which would loose legitimacy without having democratic laws like the AFSPA and Punjab Security Act 1953. Occasional patch work and cosmetic reforms apart, the deep-structured political contradictions are shelved beyond the reach of bold and visionary stroke of statesmanship, which itself is a missing word in the colonial legacy".[11]

The tangible political repercussions of the invocation of the AFSPA are hundred per cent colonial instrument, draconian law dependency, suspension of rights without proclamation of emergency and negation to center-state relationship.

It means that such historical importance could not be faced by the distorted perceptions with official projection of the Government. In short, the Government of India should understand the politico-historical basis of the upsurges. that characterise the North-Eastern life.

Examining Legislative Instruments for Counter Insurgency - AFSPA

The centre is of the view that AFSPA must stay to combat insurgency in NE states. That is why it has enacted it in order to quell the ethnic uprising in the Naga Hills in Assam in 1958. After nearly half of century, like a nuclear chain-reaction, it has spread over all the seven states of NE. But the victims of AFSPA have been all innocent citizens so far. The plain truth is: AFSPA is used or abused to kill innocent unarmed citizens rather than combating insurgency. Since its introduction in Manipur in 1961, there has never been a single case of the armed forces using this benevolent clause of AFSPA in the rescue of a kidnapped person or recovery of stolen property. AFSPA was not used against the kidnappers of Lungnila Elizabeth nor the German national who had been kidnapped while visiting Manipur. AFSPA was simply remaining as a silent spectator when the Kukis and the Nagas massacre, one another in a war of ethnic cleansing. Of what use is AFSPA against the armed gangs indulging in highway robbery in the

National Highways 39 and 53 when villages are torched, unarmed civilians killed in a contest between armed gangs? AFSPA smiles all the time knowingly to those cases. The long and the short of it, is, AFSPA with all its pious intentions is concerned with everything except civic security and order.[12]

The provision of AFSPA intrinsically is not an enabling law, but a disabling law. It cannot and should not be construed so as to mean that one's life should be taken away by enacting a law. It really negates even the procedure established by the law of the constitution. In case of protection of life and liberty of a person including a citizen Art. 21 stated that "No person shall be deprived of his life or personal liberty except according to procedure established by law".

But AFSPA can do anything in this region. Even suspicion becomes the basis of law also. It has ruled that security forces in exercise of the powers conferred by this Act is above the law of the land. S.F. may (a) fire, (b) use force, (c) kill, (d) destroy any structure, (e) arrest without warrants, (f) enter and search any house without warrant. For any action so performed, AFSPA provides blanket immunity to SF against any prosecution, suit or other legal proceedings. Section 6 of AFSPA rules out any prosecution, suit or legal proceedings against any person in respect of anything done or purported to be done in exercise of the powers conserved in this Act except with the previous sanction of the Central Government. Sanction? Why should the Government grant sanction? Had the Central Government wanted its soldiers to behave in occupying the disturbed areas, Section 6 would have been deleted altogether.[13]

The Supreme Court had disposed off the writ petition Nos. 5328 of 1980, 550 of 1982 and 9229 and 9330 of 1982, which challenged the constitutionality of the impugned black statute. On November 27, 1997 after a long span of seventeen years of receiving the petition in 1980. After accepting a set of guidelines to be followed at the time of entering the law, the apex court had upheld the validity of AFSPA-1958, the repeal of which was also desired by the chairman of the National Human Rights commission in 1996. The basic fact that the constitution does not envisage long term deployment of the armed forces in the civilian areas has been concealed.

The Supreme Court in a landmark judgment ruled that the protection given under Section 6 cannot be regarded as conferment of an immunity on the persons exercising the powers under the central Act. The apex court was of the opinion that Section 6 only gives protection in the form of previous sanction of the Central Government before a criminal prosecution or other civil proceeding is instituted against such a person. The argument is; Section 6 is not giving blanket immunity from legal prosecution as such the stipulation rather is one of necessitating prior sanction of Central Government, the absence or withdrawal of which is tantamount to blanket immunity. The principle underlying the necessity for prior sanction is simple; the Central Government's readiness to morally own or physically control the damage inflicted by the armed forces in occupation of disturbed areas is inversely proportionate to its opposition to the operation of the rule of law over the armed forces.[14]

Suppose, the Central Government refuses the state Government's request for sanction for legal prosecution against a member of the armed forces operating under AFSPA in a disturbed area, the ruling of the Supreme Court is that the order of the central Government refusing or granting the sanction is subject to judicial review and, therefore, on any count the Central Government shall pass an order giving reasons for its decision. The reasons for refusal of sanction may be judicially reviewed in the highest court of the land, namely, the Supreme Court.

AFSPA Violates the Spirit of the Constitution

In the first place, AFSPA completely negates a center-state relationship. In other words the zone of interference by the center to the state is larger. So the question of colourable legislation could be arisen.

Secondly, the two important or essential elements of democracy are liberty and equality; without which, no one can say that the people are in the democratic political system. But the people of NE are crying for right to life and equal status with other citizens of mainland India. Democracy again means rule of law, which protects life and liberty. Rule of law also protects the person against arbitrary arrest and detention. That no person shall be deprived of his life or personal liberty except according to procedure established by law (Art. 21) and also that no person who is arrested shall be detained in custody without being informed, as soon as may be, of the grounds for such arrest (Art. 22) are articles of faith in the rule of law. AFSPA gives the army the power to kill a person or arrest a person or destroy his property and home, without due process of law. This is violation of the rule of law. AFSPA therefore, violates the spirit of democracy. This strangulation of democracy in one part of the country may be the beginning for its end in the whole of the country. Experiment in suspension of democracy in the NE will have far reaching consequences for the whole of India.

AFSPA Boomeranged

AFSPA is injecting rooted tendency for the growth of a sense of alienation in collective behaviour of the Manipuri people and the region from the Indian Union. The atrocities committed by the armed forces under the cover of their Act give an impression to the mind of the common man that Manipur remains, in spite of being a full fledged state of the Indian Union, a colonial state. This impression is further re-enforced by the fact that the British Rule in India had enacted similar laws as part of its colonial rule. The Central Government should rely on political wisdom rather than military intelligence to maintain the integrity and sovereignty of the Indian Union while dealing with the states for situated from the Indian mainland. In short the use of armed forces with this act in aid of the Civil Administration further deteriorates the law and order situation instead of bringing any improvement.

Fight Against AFSPA is neither Anti-National nor Pro-Insurgent

To fight against AFSPA is neither anti-national nor pro-insurgent. You cannot kill democracy in one part of the country to maintain it elsewhere. Fight for repeal of AFSPA, is a fight in defence of democracy, freedom and right to life. It is a fight for affirmation of civil society's moral authority over brute force. It is a fight for civilization and values – against violence in all its manifestations – a way of saying "No" to the preponderance of violence in the affairs of men. We are against the armed forces of any hue, dictating the civil society what to do and what not to do. Whatever arguments made by the people of this region are the same arguments made by Pandit Nehru in 1942 against the AFSPO of the British and the reaction given by the MPs of India against the AFSPA on 18 August 1958 in Parliament.

Repealing of AFSPA and Countering Insurgency are Two Separate Issues

To repeal AFSPA conditionally on the absence or presence of insurgency is merely an argument from expediency based on the logic of the vested interest and powers that be. The argument of these vested interst that AFSPA was enacted and imposed to counter insurgency, and, that there will be no AFSPA if there is no insurgency is in reality self-defeating.

By the very logic of the argument, the operation of AFSPA for more than four decades ought to have made its impact on insurgency. But events have proved the contrary. AFSPA has proved itself counter productive in combating insurgency.

We may conclude by saying that AFSPA is an act which empowers the armed forces to have extra-judicial execution of innocent civilian populace on mere suspicion without trial by the court. Not a single law could be based on suspicion. It also amounts to conferring extra-judicial powers to the armed forces to indulging into fake encounters and custodial killings. In short, imposition of the AFSPA in NE states is a futile exercise. Rather, it has proved of having the opposite of desired effect which yields negative results. So Prof. S. Lokendra has aptly remarked that "the seed of AFSPA is British; the womb is Indian. Genetically, therefore, one can characterize AFSPA as Anglo Indian. The legal finesse is British; draconian traits oriented, rich in genetic endowments from diverse parents; AFSPA is powerfully built, as all the hybrids do. Masquerading as an enactment in defence of democracy, liberalism and integrity against terrorism, AFSPA can perpetuate state terror of the worst kind and kill democracy itself in due course".[15]

So to repeal this Act remains as a must and it will save the erosion of delicate social fabric and the people of the NE, who have already borne the burnt of the act, otherwise the people will further be alienated from the national mainstream.

Lastly, people of NE states condemned any kind of counter insurgency based on ethnic line, which engendered and heighten internal contradiction among the various ethnic groups. But today it seems to become voluminous day-by-day. Looking at the insurgency movements in Manipur, the Indian government should try to win the militants from both sides. It should not patronise one in order to neutralize the other. We had a bad experience with the Liberation Tigers of Tamil Eelam (LTTE) in Sri Lanka. In order to neutralize LTTE, India deliberately encouraged the Eelam People's Revolutionary Liberation Front (EPRLF) but history tells and warns us about how we terribly failed in our Sri Lanka's misadventure.

Now, it is high time for the centre to expedite its integrated plan of action against the insurgency alongwith an integrated socio-economic plan for the upliftment of this region. Thus,one pertinent question which invites rethinking is how can one asses that economic solutions to the present socio-economic and socio-political malady appears to be the only permanent alternative and answer to the present insurgency movement in NE states.

NOTES AND REFERENCES

1. P.C. Biswas, Insurgency in NE India: Perspective and issues, in eds., B.Pakem, *Insurgencies in NE*, India, 1997, p.224
2. Naoriya Sanajaoba,*The Genesis of Insurgencies,* in eds., Naoriya Sanajaoba, Manipur Past and Present, Delhi, 1998, p.246.
3. Sachetan Sathirth, The Nationality Question in the NE, *Symphony of Freedom,* Andhra Pradesh, 1997, p.168
4. *Report given by the Manab Adhikar Sangram Samiti.*
5. *Ibid.*
6. N. Nimai Singh, Human Rights Abuses by Security Forces in Manipur, in eds., Naorem Sanajaoba, *Human Rights*, Delhi, 1994, p.179.
7. *Resistance*, English Weekly, 11 September 1979, Imphal.
8. *CLAHRO's Report,* 1 October 1991, Imphal.
9. COHR, comp., *Human Rights Violation in Manipur,* 2005, Imphal.
10. Naorem Sanajaoba, ASPA 1958, in *The Orient Vision* ,Vol.2 Issue 1, Oct. Nov. Dec., 2004, Imphal, p.4.
11. *Ibid.*, p.3
12. Soyam Lokendrajit Singh, *Why AFSPA should be Removed*, a booklet, Imphal 2004.
13. *Ibid.*
14. *Ibid.*
15. *Ibid.*

5

CHANGING SCENARIO NATIONAL SECURITY, DEVELOPMENT AND PEACE IN THE NORTH EAST INDIA

Various scholars, administrators and journalists from the region are raising their eyebrows to see the future of insurgency in the region. Some of the organizations have already made accord with the Government like Mizo Accord. NSCN is also in the ongoing process of peace talk and there is a recent development of Bodo Accord between the major rebel groups of the Bodos and the government of Assam. On the contrary, some organisations of NE are not giving positive response when the entire state governments invite them for negotiation. So it is better to see their future. If the present writer has to see their future, it should be from the Marxist standpoint because maximum numbers of organisations are struggling with arms, based on the Marxist and the Maoist line.[1]

The Future of the Movement

Sachetan Sathirth in his 'Symphony of Freedom' subscribes his views on the future of the insurgency movement in North East India as given below: [2]

The nationality movement in the Northeast is, no doubt, a popular movement of the masses. It has been able to arouse broad sections of the masses of various nationalities against national oppression and exploitation. Despite the revolutionary spirit, dedication and heavy sacrifices of the masses, the movement is yet to be consolidated ideologically, politically and organisationally to be able to achieve its final goal.

On the ideological front, it has seen that the militant nationalist movement is being led by the left-wing sections of the petty-bourgeois classes of various nationalities. As a result of this class origin of the leadership, bourgeois nationalism is always found to prevail on the movement. The bourgeois nationalists always try to gloss over the fact that in the final analysis, the national struggle is a matter of class struggle, that national oppression is a form of class oppression. Until and unless the movement is led by a genuine proletarian leadership who follow Marxism-Leninism-Mao Tse-Tung thought as their ideology, the movement cannot achieve success and lead the people to final victory overcoming national chauvinism and sectarianism.[3]

On the political front, the movement is found to be very much weak in comparison to the strength of the enemy. The narrow outlook of the petty-bourgeois middle class leadership keeps the main ally of the movement i.e. the peasantry aloof from active participation in the movement. The leadership has failed to properly understand the democratic essence of the nationality question in modern period and so have not yet formulated any revolutionary agrarian policy and programmes of actions to attract the basic rural masses that form 80% of the population of any nationality in the region. The most important of all, indicate the true failure to examine the nationality question within the definite historical limit of the present era and the specific features of the Indian state and society on the part of leadership who has time and again adopted wrong strategy and tactics for the seizure of political power and establishment of a democratic society free from national oppression. Instead of a protracted people's war being participated mainly by the peasants and worker, they are fighting a war of quick decision by a handful of youth only resulting in the repeated destruction of the main forces at the hands of the technically superior and numerically stronger enemy having reserve forces at back and call.[4]

Secondly, there is no effective political coordination among the revolutionary nationalist organisations of the North-East region let alone coordination on an all-India or International basis. This is because of the fact that the leadership being petty-bourgeois origin has once again failed to properly understand the anti-imperialist essence of the nationality question in the present era. That under the present conditions of imperialism the nationality question in the North-East also is an international question and that the question is not an end in itself but a part of the general question of emancipation of the Indian people and the people of the whole world are almost lost sight of by the leadership. All these political weaknesses as have arisen from the wrong assessment of the concrete conditions of the Indian and world political situations.

Weak ideology and weak politics give rise to weak organisation. The revolutionary nationalist forces in the North-East are organisationally very much weak because of improper organisational line. The leadership of the nationality movement is not properly maintaining the mass line and the class line either within its own rank and file or in relation to other nationalities. As a result, the movement still remains feeble and fragmented the leadership and the rank and file being very much subjective and dogmatic.[5]

Common Views on Future of Insurgency in NE India

Some scholars had a view that regarding the future of insurgency in the NE India, it could not last long if the ongoing trend of making internal contradictions more voluminous by each group continues. It is based on the theory of contradiction of Mao Zeo Dong. According to him, one could say that the struggle is in principle antagonistic contradiction, if the oppressed class fights against the oppressor. On the contrary, if each group fights with other faction or group of their nationality, it becomes non-principle antagonistic contradiction. It is internal contradiction. Internal contradiction means the struggle is not progressing at all. One could see such internal contradictions in North East states. For instance, what is happening in the states of North East, in Assam the Assamese are fighting against the Bengalis, the Bodo against the Santhal, the Arunachali against Chakma in Arunachal Pradesh, the Mizo against the Reang in Mizoram, among the Naga and the Kuki in Manipur, and the Tripuris and the Bengalis in Tripura. Their insurgent groups are instrumental in all these internal contradictions.

Besides, internecine blood shed and fratricidal killings among the underground organisations has been occurring in Manipur since the 1980s. So, recently the proscribed KYKL calls for an end to such factional feuds through media. The organsiation states:

> *"All the differences and splits and rivalry have subsequently been ironed out. The differences could have been solved without resorting to the clashes that did nothing except led to internecine bloodshed and fratricidal killings," Further added that "History is proof that no faction can be wiped out by the stronger rival. If at all any group vanished, it is because of their own inherent weaknesses to carry on the struggle. This is a lesson that should be learnt by all".*[6]

Another important factor which limited the progress of struggle of North East is that there is no common political aspiration among them. The Assamese talk about the Assamese only, the Naga inserts their interest only, the Kukis for Kukis, the Tripuris for only the Tripuris. Each group always asserts their own interest for the sake of themselves. Such assertion always invites reaction from others. As a consequence of it, t the people of NE still cannot have a common political aspiration.It could not be possible in future also until and unless there is common political socialisation.

Stressing on the importance of unity among the people, especially amongst the armed groups operating in Manipur, the Chairman of KYKL, Achou Toijamba said on 11th foundation day of his organisation which falls on 25th April 2005 that "the time has come for all underground outfits to talk things over and find a common route to their goal."

While addressing the people on the eve of the Foundation Day, the KYKL leader admitted that the failure of the numerous underground outfits to forge a united struggle is the biggest drawback in the struggle to regain the lost sovereignty of the land and people.

Further he observed that "the lack of unity amongst the armed groups has also eroded the trust and confidence of the people in the armed movement. Though the learned and the educated people may acknowledge the validity of the goals and aspirations of the armed movement, the very conduct of the armed cadres have stopped them from coming out and supporting the movement added the statement."[7]

Nationalism Versus Ethnonationalism and its Impact in Future of Movement

No one can affford to be a Cyclops by perceiving the concept of racial boundary. If he or she opens the chapter of racial boundary as consequence why should not America merges to Britain, Jammu and Kashmir to Pakistan, Pakistan to Iran, Bengal to Bangladesh and North East people to either Myanmar or Thailand. Not only the cited races, but also maximum nations of the world should have been in the national reorganization process. So by using political wisdom, the ruling elites and intellectuals of the world did not keep their nations in peril and not in dangling position. That means they closed the chapter of racial boundary with daring determination. Very much contrary to this, in NE, some racial groups are at stake in the romantic revere of day-dreaming with extreme interpretation of racial boundary. So, the question of the emergence of ethnic army, ethno-nationalism and internal enemies arose and thus forcefully created victims. These victims become the ethnic armies and then the killers. These are the impact of ethno-nationalism and of having faith in the idea of racial boundary.

Nationalism and Ethnonationalism

Nationalism is not a new phenomenon. In fact, most

modern nations have developed gradually on the basis of common descent and ties of ethnic, religious and linguistic character which led to the creation of a feeling of belonging to a community living in a certain territory. The tendency towards nationalism was fostered mainly by various political, cultural, economic and technological developments. As a distinctive movement, nationalism emerged in the eighteenth and nineteenth centuries and can be seen as an important factor in the building of nation-states. In itself, it is not necessarily a negative phenomenon, and may also be a positive phenomenon. In this sense it is perhaps more appropriate to use the term 'patriotism', which helped to keep nations together in the most difficult periods of their history.

These senses of nationalism, belongingness, and patriotism could not tie up the heart and minds of the people of the North East because of their historical importance and historical rights. So, the passing of the twentieth century brings new challenges, its character is often articulated in a form of aggressive or extreme nationalism which is often linked to the "right to self-determination (external)."

Sources of Extreme and Aggressive Nationalism

What are the sources of the present explosion of extreme, aggressive nationalism? There are many politically coercive centre dominated consensus of the masses and economically exploited too. In short, still they claim that they are in the colonial yolk. So, decolonization is the crux of the issue. As concrete evidence, one could witness national liberation movement with violent methods. It has been in continuation is being continued since the 1950s till now.

Creation of Internal contradiction

As measures of combating liberation movement, ethno-nationalism is injected to the feeble minds of the various ethnic groups, which leads to internal ethnic conflicts and massive and flagrant abuse of human rights such as genocide in Rwanda or ethnic cleansing in former Yugoslavia. Ethno-nationalism can be characterized as a tendency either to achieve a hegemonic position for a given ethnic group in a heterogeneous society or to secede from it. In order to achieve a dominant position, ethno-nationalists utilize either forced assimilation, imposition of a dominant cultural identity, language and religion or exclusion of members of other ethnic groups from the national society by the denial and deprivation of citizenship or by outright ethnic cleansing.

It may also have a form of discrimination directed against other groups in multicultural societies – immigrants or indigenous peoples – and is used by a state, seen as a 'property' of one ethnic group, in order to achieve greater cohesion or consolidation of a dominant ethnic group by the creation of images of 'internal enemies'. Ethno-nationalistic movements have a strong irrational component which contributes to their strength but at the same time makes them less susceptible to political compromise or acceptance of the rights of other cultural groups. It leads in some cases to the issue of various forms of violence and terrorism by forming ethnic army. Their demands are mainly the rights to internal self-determination, autonomy, presentation and participation in decision-making processes in state institutions, in political, economic, social and cultural development with arms movement in character.[8]

From the above views regarding nationalism, sub-nationalism and ethno-nationalism, we come to understand that Indian nationalism creates the tendencies of having sub-nationalism to the people of NE and ethno-nationalism as countering such tendencies automatically, comes up to make confusion of the newly emerging sub-nationalisms which are demanding with external self-determination. The current tendency of ethno-nationalism has entered an ominous stage, where the use of violence and coercion has added new dimensions to ethnic politics. The varying degree of ethnic assertion and its success in securing various level of self rule, including statehood and redrawing of state boundaries on the basis of ethnic considerations in the region has almost institutionalized the ethnification process in spite of some organizations considering them as oppressed class.

Logic Behind the Ethnic States or Racial Boundaries

Their logic and discontentment which distorted the common political aspiration of NE are that the creation of 'ethnic' states may have satisfied the bigger communities, such as Assam for the Assamese, Arunachal for the Arunachalis, Nagaland for the Nagas, Mizoram for the Mizos, but it failed to accommodate the smaller communities and tribes, which remained embedded within the larger ethnic groupings of the respective states, all of which contain a multi-ethnic constellation of populations. Ironically, the existing democratic systems primarily function through the representatives of majority population located within a politico-administrative territory in a state. The wishes and aspirations of the minority communities are often ignored; they find themselves completely marginalized in areas where they do not form a majority. The second stage autonomy movements of the Bodo, Karbis, Dimasas, Kochrajbanshis, Tai Ahoms, Missings, among others in Assam; Hmars and Reangs in Mizoram clearly explain this.

Moreover, state boundaries have been drawn up in such a way that they often cut through the socio-cultural boundaries of certain communities, destroying their natural habitation. The plight of the Reangs (living on both the sides of Mizoram – Tripura boundaries), the Chakmas (divided between Chittagong Hill Track (CHT) of Bangladesh and Indian state of Mizoram), the Kuki-Chin tribes (scattered in continuous states of south Assam, Mizoram and Manipur and across the chin state of Myanmar), the Nagas (separated between Indian Nagaland and Western Myanmar), the Khasis and the Garos (scattered in Assam and across Bangladesh), is the result of this artificial division. The complete marginalisation of the indigenous communities through relentless influx of more organized immigrant Bengali community in Tripura is another terrible story. Naturally, most of these communities have resorted to arms to secure their homeland, when they realized that they had little chances to retain control over the resources, or at least ensured of their share of it, within the areas where they became minority.[9]

These different demands and aspirations of the various groups, when, compounded with people's movement without streamlining the movement, it becomes confused day by day. So we have to distinguish clearly nationalism, sub-nationalism and ethno-nationalism. Moreover we have to identify the group which is demanding internal self-determination and external self-determination. Moreover, we have to have very clear demarcation in between ethnic army and national liberation army. Otherwise, branding of different names will create more and more confusion.

Really speaking, the people of NE are not in the position of concrete class structure i.e. oppressed people as a whole in spite of launching class struggle in between oppressed people and oppressor. Collectively, they did not understand that the variation and differentiation were created by the capitalist system when they were in the participant political culture. The privileged groups, belonging to any communities or ethnic groups, were in the higher strata of society and others were marginalized. There is no question of high caste and low caste, general and tribal, Hinduism and Christianity. Even there are good numbers of well-to-do families in the tribal communities. But, on the other hand, the general category people living in remote areas are lagging far behind and backward in all fields. These are the results of our existing capitalist economy and unmeaningful democratic political system having feudal and colonial character. Instead of giving maximum reaction to uproot the system, in order to bring socialism for radical transformation, the people of North East are inactive because of the existing system. But they always try to see all these through ethnic angles. So they become the pointed rod at which all ethnic groups are joining as pieces of meat on the fire. The notable thing is who shoots you and makes into pieces and keeps on fire for food?"[10]

For whose good: National Security, Peace and Development

The discourse on peace and development in North-East India becomes a hot cake to day. It is always associated with the question of national security also. But one notable thing is that it could not serve the purpose by projection of distorted perception of peace and development. Basically if there are social security, political security and economic security, we won't need to talk about national security, because individuals are the units of the state and the states are the units of the nation. Why do we impute the blame on the emergence of dissent groups? Disagreement, on the ground of principle, is a healthy process of development. However, if the objective of dissent is positive, it encourages the individuals and the institutions to take positive step to drive home the authority for correction of omission and commission. In fact, they do not make denial of positive content. Even we have to arraign destruction though they have total indifference from positive contention. By keeping these views in our minds, it is better to see the correct perception of security, peace and development in the positive way and the need for how it could be put into practice.

Concept of Security

Let us start by noting that the term "concept" in the phrase "concept of security" is ambiguous in an important way. In a more narrower and philosophical sense, to define a concept is tantamount to giving the meaning of a term or of a phrase, e.g. by producing synonyms that have the same connotations. In a wider sense, however, the term "concept" may connote much more, including, the methods or strategies. In particular, when we speak about "concept of security", explaining somebody's concept in the philosophical sense only involves making it clear how he uses the term "security" and giving a translation of that term into some other terms. In the wider sense, explaining somebody's concept of unity involves describing the major lines of action, or strategies that are employed in achieving security: how he thinks about security in a much broader sense than formal definition.

We see that those two senses of "concept of security" are widely different, and to avoid linguistic confusion, we have to refer to the philosophical sense of "concept", whereas the term "conception" will be used for the broader sense. The two senses are obviously related in a number of ways. The most important of these is that in order to discuss whether the conception of security that a state (or any other actor) entertains is, in fact, likely to enhance his security or how it is likely to affect the security of other actors, we first have to know what concept of security, he and the others, have.

Search for Definitions

The term "security" in English, as well as its translations into most other languages is strongly and positively valve-loaded. These valve connotations to the word mean that the "rules of language" make it more or less axiomatic that "security is good", even if that does not mean that it is the highest valve. For this reason, at least one aspect of any discussion over adequate definitions of "security" will regard with which content to associate these positive value connotations. In particular; the discussion is not an academic one but an attempt by two or several actors to arrive at a common definition. Then a necessary condition for agreement will be that there is at least some degree of value consensus among the actors.

As a consequence of this, national sovereignty appears to be important in relation to definition of "security". More concretely, since there is considerable variation in the goals and priorities among them in the international system and since one of the value connotations of the term "security" is that "security is legitimate", each state may be expected to regard itself as the final judge of how to define "security", in addition to regarding itself as the final judge of by what means to achieve or preserve security. The former point presumes that states have interests in getting precisely their goals, or some subset of them, sanctified by being subsumed under the umbrella-term "security". They will, therefore, often disagree, Major powers may include preservation of spheres of interest under "security", whereas other states will not, some states may include development goals in "security", and others will see such goals as falling outside that concept, etc.

The term "security" is used to connote concepts on various levels: whereas "national security" (normally meaning security of a state) is a common and frequent phrase, it is by no means the only context in which the term "security" appears! Sometimes it connotes characteristics or states of affairs of various sub-national entities, including individual human beings, and sometimes the entities referred to are more encompassing, such as alliances, regions or even the international system in its entirety. There is not a priori ground to assume that the term "security" must have the same meaning in all these different contexts. Even if governments are the ultimate judges of how to define the security of their own states, this does not mean that they should not make their definitions increasingly explicit, for example, in dialogue with each other. Such a dialogue might at least serve the purpose of making states more sensitive to the differences in definitions, to the security needs seen by other states, and to how their own security arrangements are seen to relate to these. Nor does it necessarily exclude that public debates inside states could improve given concepts of security, so as to lead to more rational and informed policies of security.

Finally, it makes an important point in a different direction; not only is the notion of security a many-dimensional one, it also has to deal with different levels and with the relations between them. In particular, it is important to try to identify how many meanings in common there are between people's security and national security and how they are otherwise logically related to each other.[11]

Social Security Crux of National Security

From the foregoing survey of various difficulties generally the question is ask if "security" could be defined in any possible way. In our present discourse we need to stress more and more to the individuals. That means we have to start with the level of human beings, and how "security" can be delimited on this level, one essential component of human security is, of course, security against direct physical violence, whether inflicted by other individuals or groups, by parts or agents of the state machinery, or by attacks from other states. While this can be seen as a necessary condition for stating that an individual is enjoying security, it is definitely not a sufficient condition. Many definitions will also include protection of the liberty and various civil rights of the individual. Furthermore, an individual who is not able to satisfy his basic human needs, such as food, clothes, housing, health, education and work, can hardly be regarded as enjoying security according to other definitions of that concept, even if the subset of them that are included may vary somewhat, depending on what definition we look at; at least, most of these needs are usually covered by the term "social security". Truly speaking, analysis of national security could not be possible by isolating it from the individual level. Thus the state usually appears as a protector of at least some aspects of human security, it may also define a threat, e.g. in connection with conflicts over the control of the state machinery, or when the individual is inducted to serve in the armed forces of the state in military conflicts with other actors.

From this present discussion, we come to understand that if there is no individual security in social, political and economical spheres there exists basically threats to the territorial integrity of the nation and to the political institutions and system of the nation. But, for this reaction, the state could not make official projection, considering that aspiration by polarising distorted concept, threats to the development and economic welfare of the state. So the question of survival and transformation is in conical flask of laboratory.[12]

Peace and Development

The twin basic national problems in connection with north-eastern states are survival and transformation or to put it in conventional language, peace and development. Both are inextricably interlinked and the future hinges on their healthy growth. But it is not possible without thorough planning and permanent observation of the centre. It also could not be treated only as an economic factor when we discuss the problems of North East states. It is easy to point out a number of social problems which would remain, or even get worse, if the engine of growth got started again. The most important aspects of these are:

1. marginalization
2. the social crisis
3. legitimation crisis.

The term "marginalisation" means the transfer of people to the fringes of society. They loose their function in the system and become superfluous. They also feel unwanted and, as a consequence, lose their self-respect; unemployment is only one form of marginalization. Part of the youths is marginalized; they are the ones who are simply stored in schools because they have no place in the labour market. Old people are retired on pensions even though they would like to continue to lead an active life. Over and above, the people of North East are confronted with the problem of migration, which leads into demographic imbalance. So the people of this region are very much worried for their future. In short there is no future for them.

The second problem which remains is even if we manage to get out of the economic predicament, it is still the social crisis. The emergence of ethnicity creates sectarianism and chauvinism. Each of the ethnic groups always asserted their own interest while jeopardizing the interest of others. So assertion and reaction become the conflict and it turns also as spiral conflict culture. This is also the outcome of creating non-principle antagonistic contradiction in order to suppress the principle antagonistic contradiction of the underground movement.

Moreover, there are contradictions between the established major religious groups like Hinduism and the revivalist of indigenous culture and religion of this region. The present generation is, really, in struggle to pass out from the frozen layers of forced assimilation in the past. Besides, in every house husband and wife are at stake to defend challenges of immature feminist movements, its framework planted from western countries. It is complete doggerel but effusion among them. In short one could see both macro and micro level internal contradictions in the region. It is also very much voluminous and increasing day by day. Maximum number of population both men and women have no permanent and stable economic status.

Moreover, talented young people have to move to the industrial growth pools outside the region which are completely cut off from the industrial map in the North East states. Thus they lost contact with their parents, relatives, former friends and neighbours. So, such conditions upturn their social environment to a new critical social relationship. People are transformed into passive, isolated consumers of private goods and public services. They cannot do much by themselves, and so, a number of social problems arises. Isolated people cannot take care of themselves if they get sick; they are apt to seek consolation in alcohol and drugs. Another gloomy picture of the youth of this region is that they are counting the days of their death because of having HIV positive and living with AIDS. They are the victims of counter revolutionary movement. Both the Union and state governments are seen to giving syringes to their hands in order to take away guns from their hands. This big burden is on the head of all the elders of the family members of this region.

The third problem may be called the legitimate crisis. What we call "development" lacks a firm legitimate basis. We have lost our belief in the myths that once gave meaningful value to the great industrial projects. The legitimate crisis has many components. There is a crisis of confidence; the loyalty of the citizens to the political system is decreasing. There is also a crisis of motivation; quite a few people have lost all desire to perform the alienating roles of production and consumption that are required of them in a technological society.

Mistrust in governments is only one indicator of a general decline of confidence in authority figures. In 1970, for instance 25 percent of the NE people argued that one cannot "trust the government doing what, is right". Thirty-four years later 75 percent endorse the same statement. There is much talk about contempt for politicians but the crisis of confidence also hits company managers, union bosses, government officials, scientific experts and religious hands. The only elites without faults in the mind of the people are those in the teaching prosession of higher educational institutions. They never demand money when their students pursue them to take more classes. They seem to understand, they are paid for their service to the students. All the others both temporary and permanent executives, are demanding money for discharging their concerned duties in the offices.

Another indicator of decreasing trust is the frequency of party changes before implementing the anti defection law. Since 1972 Manipur has been having a rather unstable party and government. So the maximum electorate have no party loyalty and are not party oriented. More and more voters have lost faith in the ability of their party and its leaders to solve political problems. Hence, they are now searching for alternatives.[13]

Models of Development

The North Eastern States of India are lagging far behind in development despite their vast potentials; the untapped hydel power (not mega dam), mineral resources, virgin forests, sturdy people and water resources of the region could change the face of the region. Lack of development (social, political and economic development of the individuals) has brought about a sense of neglect and frustration among the people. Young people are feeling alienated and getting restless. For them development means meeting the needs of the present generation without jeopardizing the needs of the future generation. So they ask so often, "development for whom"? It should be development of all not for a particular handful of people.

In the development process there is the tendency of depending upon money power rather than on real economic growth. Plethora of money is spent in the NE states without corresponding fundamental change in the production structure. In the north-eastern states, being in a special category, Central Government fund flows not always in proportion. This has resulted in demoralizing the administration and the people. Money allocated for social welfare activities, partly goes to the poor but largely to the privileged few. Social values of dedication and commitment to the society have largely been eroded and are replaced by greed and personal aggrandisement. The socializing virtues of the tribal society is yielding place to individual and self-seeking opportunism. Being in special category, almost the entire expenditure of these states is run by the Central Government. One result is that the people do not have to bear the corresponding cost of the benefit they are enjoying. State governments, on the other hand, have very limited financial strength. State revenue being very low, the expenditure of the state governments, mainly for administrative purposes, is met by central fund. The easy money thus flowing in the state has also made the state administrative sector almost parasitic and inefficient.

A long-term strategy for the development of the region will be meaningless unless this region prepares itself for such economic integration with the neighbouring economics. Its internal preparedness is crucial for benefits from mutual trade and travels. In the beginning it has been pointed out that the whole understanding of North-East's resource complex is misplaced, which needs reassessment; without such a review it may not be feasible to make important strategic internal changes. What construes the natural resources of the region? It has fertile land both in the valleys and hills and forested tracts of immense beauty and rich bio-diversity. It has water both, flowing – plenty of it and the potential hydro power resources. It has people with their variegated cultures, skills and generally, a highly literate pool of manpower that is little used because of lack of employment opportunities. It has the forests and the biological (and genetic) resource pool. The resource complex, therefore, is not the dead minerals but a living pool of resources. Its development strategy must, therefore, be based on this living complex of resources, not necessarily industrialization understood in the common parlance. It does not mean here that the other industries like oil and petro-chemicals or coal or limestone based industries are to be discouraged. It does mean more in changing the emphasis on the direction of development.[14]

It will need a new blue-print. So mention could be made of the suggestions given by Mohapatra. They are:

(1) A strategic shift emphasising in agriculture (crop farming) in the valleys from monsoon based practices (which may continue) do irrigation based farming during the off seasons. This region has one of the least irrigated areas of the country, since the traditional monsoon farming was considered adequate – irrigation was not promoted. From the farmers' point of view, monsoon not only provides water for the rice paddies, it also brings in the floods and the concomitant risks on investments. Flood protection, though it is necessary it can neither be effectively controlled in the same manner as in other areas of the country, nor is desirable due to the sheer volume of discharge from the region. An effective alternative appears to be the dry-season farming. This of course, needs substantial public investments as well as promoting private investments in irrigation. Agriculture can then yield a livelihood and may absorb a good proportion of the idle manpower.

The region is currently a food deficit zone. Its farming practices, crop calendar changes are enabled by irrigation. In a decade's time the region can turn the corner and become food surplus. But it may not gain comparative advantage vis-à-vis other grain farming areas of the country due to high transportation costs. This is when opening of links with the neighbouring region of the South-East Asia become handy. However, rice will not enjoy a comparative advantage in those regions where there is surplus production (Thailand and Myanmar, e.g.) and which are technologically superior and more efficient. A change in mixed production will be necessary. Trade and travel will bring in demonstration effect on the farming practices, since the agro-climatic conditions of the North-East are much closer to the South-East Asia than mainland India and thus, farming practices and technologies of that region will be more effective in the North-East than the current practices promoted.

(2) In the hills, however, the strategy need not be grain farming, but complex of silviculture, horticulture, and animal husbandry, may be taken up which wherever initiated have yielded excellent results.

(3) There must be accentuated research and development of plant-genetic resources of the region and promotion of economic species at the field level. This also needs appropriated documentation and patenting of genetic resources.

(4) The region also needs re-working of its manpower development from general education to professional and vocational programmes and skill upgradation programmes including farmers training for the suggested package strategy. Though a good literacy situation is an adequate starting point, it may not be enough without appropriate filtering of skills right down to the grass root level.

(5) The region ought to promote its natural and cultural heritage as a marketable product. This

again requires public and private investments in tourism development and skill upgradations in tourist services. The region can also promote its traditional products like cottage textiles with their wonderful designs and motifs as exportable commodities. Specialized designing and training centres will be essential. Though this is being done to some extent now, it is not enough and more specialized inputs and governmental support may be necessary.

(6) There would also be the need for internal liberalisation within the region before any external integration is thought of. External integration would require free movement, investment decisions and property ownership. Under the current liberalization strategy and industrial promotion programmes in the region (Tax holiday e.g.) hardly any investment has flowed into the region principally because there are many restrictive laws prevalent. Investors abhor restrictions on their decision to invest – where to invest and what to invest. Without internal liberatlisation, external integration and export promotion will remain a distant dream.

(7) There would also be the need for considering and giving more emphasis to the informal sector for the economic development of the region. It was experimented in Nordic countries and got benefit of informal economy.[15]

Whenever we are in the discourse on development in case of NE India, we have got various paradigms of development in the interaction in between the people and the government. They are – Imperialism as Development,

Anti imperialism as development, Anti-centrism-cum-separatism as development, nation's integration as development, nationalist versus cultural development paradigm, development versus sustainable development. All these inputs of development should be chanalised in the dialectics of state and civil society. After that we will get the real output. It could also be in the process of feedback loof if the environment defies them. As reaction, if the government understands development in the real sense, one will have to either deconstruct or negate the civil society oriented development paradigm; otherwise who could see their future. So as Mohapatera rightly remarked "The choice is to be with the people – whether a more liberal, integrative outlook on development or an inward looking perspective that may keep the region in the morass of backwardness, poverty and unemployment. If an inward looking nation like Japan could break open (1858) and become a superpower in no time, why the North-East could not become prosperous? It has the means – it needs the will."

Lastly, now our discourse on peace is also paradoxical. Mention has been made in the sense that before 1980 there was full of peace in NE India but no development was there. Even to day Arunachal is a land of peace and harmony but no development could be seen in comparison with others states of NE. So it is not true to say that development will certainly be there if there is peace.[16] Some are of the view that the states of North East India are in the process of development after armed struggle have been launched. People also want the solution to come by political dialogue not by military means. People of the North East have been witnessing the existence of deadly conflicts. It is defined as organized violence that kills large number of individuals. It includes war among the states and war or genocide within the states. But in using this shorthand, most thoughtful proponents of this objective do not seek peace at any price. "Prevention of conflict" includes an unstated, and often unacknowledged, measures of "justice" and "freedom". Consider China's programme that is successfully "preventing deadly conflict" in Tibet today. It succeeded by effectively suppressing basic rights of the Tibetan population. Nowhere does Tibet appears as a successful case of preventing deadly conflict nor should it. Until recently, president Slobodan Milesovic pursued a similar approach to preventing deadly conflict in Kosovo. Serbian authorities denied basic rights to the 99 per cent of the population who are Albanians. The outbreak of violence in March 1998 shows that such policies are not only unjust, but also unsustainable.

The tension between "order" on the one hand, and "freedom" and "justice" on the other, is one of the oldest themes in political theory. It is said, "We seek peace at the expense of freedom, but not both peace and freedom". That is the same case that the people of the North East want to have fundamental freedom and do not like to question about right to life. Moreover, they want to have the real taste of rule of law.

Peace Process in the NE India

The following pattern emerges from governmental initiatives for peace in the North-East.

i. Un-conditional denial of the demand for complete sovereignty or the right to self-determination.

ii. Using developmental initiatives for particular

schemes to create the context of peace has been a constant theme in the centre's policy on conflict resolution in the North-East. Since 1996, billions of Rupees have been announced as special packages for the North-East.

iii. Poor implementation of each and every government programmes, including the special packages continues to create beneficiaries of conflict.

iv. Surrender of a section of militants and another section continuing to flee.

v. Breaking of existing states and Re-organisation of states.[17]

From this Governmental initiative for peace in the North East states, we came to understand that Government is using developmental initiative to create the context of peace as a constant theme and cream for negotiating with underground organization, there is possibility of altering the existing boundary of the state. That means the gun-fighting in between the underground militants and the security forces will be stopped but it invites fighting among the various communities. Can we accept it as the constructive peace process? In case of development by pouring in huge amount of money as economic package, will it be meaningful for the development of all? It would be for a few people; they are the ministers and their relatives and the bureaucrats. So the question will remain in the minds of the people forever, and that is "Development for Whom"?

NOTES AND REFERENCES

1. I. Chaoren, *Eina Yaon Lambigi Khongul Libada*.The author who is the Chairman of the proscribed RPF whose armed wing is PLA, stated that his organisation is struggling with arms based on the basis of the ideological doctrines of Marxism, Leninism and Maoism.
2. Sachetan Sathirth, The Nationality Question in NE, in *Symphony of Freedom,* Andhra Pradesh, 1996 pp.164-165.
3. *Ibid.,* p.164.
4. *Ibid.,* p.165.
5. *Ibid.,* p.166.
6. Statement issued by the KYKL, *The Sangai Express*, 3 February 2005.
7. *Ibid.*
8. Sanat K. Chakrabaty, Wanted: An Ethnic Vision for North East, in *Grassroots Options* 2002/03, p.12.
9. *Ibid.*, p13.
10. Dhanabir Laishram, Ethno-nationalism and its Impact in the Contemporary Politics of NE, *The Imphal Free Press,* 26 January 2005, Imphal, p.2.
11. Hakan Wiberg, Concepts of Security: A Logical and Analytical Framework, in eds.,Narindar Singh, *Peace and Development,* Lancer Press, Delhi, 1988, p.32.
12. *Ibid.*, p.33.
13. *Ibid.*, p.36.
14. A.C. Mohapatra, Development and Underdevelopment of the North East Region: Search for a paradigm, in eds.,Bimal, J. Deb, *Development Priorities in NE India*, Concept Publishing Co., New Delhi, 2002, p.28.
15. *Ibid.*, p.29.
16. Dr. RK. Nimai, Ways and Means for Economic Development in Manipur, paper presented in the Seminar on *Development and Peace,* organised by Editors' Forum, Manipur, at State Guest House, Imphal on 28-29 October 2004,
17. *Pages of People's Voice,* Vol.4 number 2, April-June 2004, published by ROE Units & CSD.

6

CONCLUSION

For the present armed struggle of the North East region generally each group blames the other. For instances, the opposition parties blames the ruling party, the ruling party blames the opposition parties, the state police blames the army, the para-military, and the central government blames the state government and the militants. Government of India never recalled their past political process towards North-East i.e., isolation model and assimilation and force assimilation. So it is an undisputed fact that, for this present crisis, the government of India is responsible because of its lopsided policy towards the problems of the north east. Moreover, right from the beginning all the predecessor governments in India did not have thorough policy and permanent observation to these states. They had no clear cut policy towards the insurgents of the North East. In short its attitude and policy can be described as "ad-hoc" policy and casual observation.

So, the question of being in a Benthic zone can be raised. Generally, we come to understand that a Benthic zone is the deep sea of the oceanic region. It is pitch dark and characterisaed by universal absence of light in this environment any possibility of any growth of vegetation or other photosynthetic organisms is reuled out.

Consequently, most of the deep-sea dwellers depend upon the detritus (dead body and excreta of surface forms) which sink in to the sea bottom while a large number of species are active predators (carnivores). However the deep ocean benthos are surprisingly diverse. Food is a little more plentiful on the bottom than it is in the deep waters of the ocean, because the sediments are the ultimate resting place for all the detritus raining out of the plentiful on the bottom than it is in the deep waters of the ocean out of the upper layers. All the benthos are having their own ray to search their foods. Metaphorically, the the fate of the people of North-East India lies in the same Benthic jone. It is the alleged handiwork of the centre. So, the people of the North East are politically in the Benthic zone. As consequence, violence is taken up by them as their desired means with arms as the ray for their survival and to brinhg radical transformation and complete emancipation from the political, economic, social, cultural and all other kinds of bondage.

The people of North East are facing the problems of forced assimilation, loss of their ancestral land, lots of internal conflicts, and captive market economy. The Indian constitution is biased against the North East states. Even they cannot own their land and their resources. So the people of the North East mainly the youngsters, began to assert a separate political identity different from the Indian mainland, and resorted to armed struggle against, what they perceived, 'Indian hegemony'. They brought out the issue of language, the ethnic origin (Mongoloid stock), religion and belief system to articulate their distinctiveness. Besides, new demands are being articulated by the different tribes and the ethnic groups covering the entire range in respect of language, medium, cultural preservation, autonomy and creation of ethnic states. It leads to voluminous internal contradictions. It has been tactically used as a very effective counter insurgency measures to suppress the political aspirations of each groups. It also destroys the ground for common political aspirations. On the other hand leaders of the ethnic groups conceive the idea that ethnicity play a key role in shaping the struggle for self-determination (internal) of their diverse tribal and indigenous community. At the core, all these ethnic assertions lie the cardinal issue of (1) security of life and livelihood; (2) resources and bio diversity on which certain people survive; and lastly (3) control over the territories including the socio-cultural boundaries, which they regarded as their inalienable living space.

Another inflammable and sensitive issue coming up is inter-ethnic conflicts based on territorial demands. It leads to redrawing of state boundaries on the basis of ethnic considerations. It is the root cause of ethnic tensions, killings and large-scale dislocation of people.

According to Professor Gangmumei Kamei, a renowned historian, conflict is inevitable in a plural society. Yet, there is co-existence of cultural groups when the elites of the cultural segments make alliance and collaboration to have equal access to the state and its resources. And these competing ethnic groups have ultimately made the state resources and distributors of resources, a source and promoter of new values. The state assumes a pre-dominant role in a plural society. In a democratic system, the representatives of the people control the state mechanism and manage the government utilizing state power. But, the problem is that the state can't implement any policy for the betterment of the masses because of having legitimation crisis of ruling elites and having large area of zone of interference by the central government.

Basically, insurgent movement or national liberation movement with arms, whatever may be, is the outcome of the existing political and economic system. It is said that if there is exploitation, there will be revolution. So, bringing a solution will be beneficial to both the armed groups and the general public. The government of India should also come 'forward to contain the movement in the various phases of retrogression of insurgency, phases of stabilisation of recovery and development in order to get retrogressive changes. It has been going on through four phases like psychological phase, political phase, military phase and mobilisation phase. Some of the aims to accelerate the process of retrogression of insurgency to be achieved are given below (government of India seems to take this process in the North East India):

1. Strong political will, firm determination, resources and commitment/ ability of the government to defeat the insurgents by eliminating their recruiting base and out-maneuvering them in their territory and rehabilitating surrenderees but not accusing them of specific crimes.

2. Unified commands at various levels to co-ordinate social, political, economic, and military actions taken up to defeat insurgents.

3. To win the hearts and minds of the local people by psychological warfare and other socio-economic and administrative measures enabling the majority of the local people to have maximum of food, cloth and shelter, irrespective of discrimination. Because poverty is a greater enemy than external

disturbances. Also the protection of local people has to be ensured.

4. During military operations, army, paramilitary forces and police including "intelligence organization" should act in co-ordination. Keeping the overall national perspective and human values in view should act in the most cordial manner.
5. Counter insurgents must act within the framework of law with human approach.
6. Physical and moral fitness and ideological orientation of the counter insurgency forces are essential.
7. Task must be finished and all actions must be taken to their logical conclusion. It must be remembered that there is no short cut means to counter-insurgency and the action once started, must be taken to its logical conclusion.

This retrogression process of insurgency is given by R.N. Prasad (B. Pakem's Insurgency in North East India p.66). But could not be applied by our security forces, the ruling government and the bureaucrats. So they become anti people. For instance, after torturing and killing innocent people, they distributed food, cloths and other essential commodities to villagers at the spot areas. Moreover, they are not moral and ideological oriented. All of their actions are not based on humanitarian approach. So during operation, security forces are completely out of keeping the overall national perspective and human values, and do not act in a cordial manner. That means they cannot get two important aspects in the process of retrogression of insurgency, these are development administration and political settlement.

Then R.N. Prasad further gives some indirect steps to be taken up to restore normalcy at the time of retrogression of Insurgency. They are given below:

1. Increase in constitutional political activities in the population.
2. Increase involvement of people in economic development and long term planning and change of economy towards industrialisation.
3. People start merging with national mainstream of life.
4. Pattern of agriculture changes towards permanent and better producing system.
5. Community and health development.
6. Improvement in education facilities and increase in number of students.
7. Change in social customs, eating habits, marriage and courtship patterns.
8. Strengthening of the administrative set up.
9. Improvement of communication facilities .
10. Economic development, changes in lifestyles, standard of living and attitude towards future.
11. Outside groups lost interest in insurgency.
12. Mobilization in public opinion.

As a matter of fact, the benefits of these retrogressive changes hardly reach the poorest and oppressed section of society. It is clearly because the role which the state can play in promoting the radical, social development measures and socio economic justice, would depend upon the class character of state power in India. The nature of the state, in turn, would depend upon the mode of production and the classes, which own the means of production, and it is in the interest of this class that state power shall be exercised. Hence, it would be futile to expect the Indian state to promote land reforms, socio-economic justice and social development measures genuinely, which would hit at a very base of power of the ruling elite. Considering the character of the political power structure obtaining in the country, it is only natural that the required political will is not forthcoming. Until and unless, a political party representing the class interest of the poor and the landless peasants comes to power both at the center and states, no effective implementation of land reform, socio-economic justice and social development measures can be expected. For example Bimal Basu, chairman of All India Communist Marxist comes so often to Manipur and other Northeast states to study all the issues and give voice to the center in a very constructive way. It indicates that he and his party are at stake to articulate the aspiration of the marginalized people of the peripheries in comparison with other national parties.

Besides centralised socio-economic planning, the process of decision-making and the manner and extent of central involvement in state subjects have created new tensions in center-state relationship. The state is perceived more and more as an instrument of coercion. This is inevitable with increasing over centralization of political, economic, judicial powers and educational and media policies. There is a need for more effective use of National Development Council. A meaningful consultation with the state at different levels is essential at every subsequent stages in the framing of the detailed plan. There is financial domination of the centre which operate in various ways. There is a need for decentralised planning along with a well developed system of information feedback to the centre so that major deviation from essential priorities or substantial-shortfalls in performance can come to the notice promptly and remedial measures can be adopted in time to be effective for future. There is also a need to strengthen the state council for solving inter-state disputes and to strengthen the cooperation among the states. What the present author wants to emphasize is that the development strategy must not be seen as merely the formulation of a new economic strategy. It has to be concerned with all the different dimensions of social relations in India today.

Even the political restructuring of the present system has to be considered. The perspective has also to involve the people in the solution of their own problems. All that is necessary to accelerate the process of stabilizing recovery and development of all types of adopting egalitarian means and values and democratic socialist arrangements should be involved.

These can be put into practice only when the government's agencies have sincerity and firm determination. Otherwise, emphasis to direct steps taken by the security forces to suppress the movement and torturing of the people is supposed to invite people's war. In connection with it, one could recall that what was really happening in 2000 and 2004 in Manipur Cease Fire's Extension and their movement against AFSPA. Moreover, the government should not instigate extension of internal contradictions as part of counter insurgency.

Constitutional Protection

Some scholars often question, why they, the Northeasterners often engaged in violent confrontations and bloodshed instead of seeking democratic dialogue to solve their problems. It seems to be conceiving the idea that they have no opportunity to participate in national decision making on the ground that they have only two or one representatives in the parliament while Uttar Pradesh sends as many as 85 representatives in the Lok Sabha. So accommodation of their asserted interest in the space of constitution is the only thing, which is demanded by the prevailing situation of the region.

Land and Resources should be Owned by the People

If we study carefully all the constitutional provisions under various articles of the Indian constitution, we will find that some of the provisions are biased against Manipur and the Northeastern states. The economic backwardness and the political discontentment of the North East cannot be removed unless the constitution is transformed radically. For example, the constitutional provisions dealing with the exemptions from taxation by states in respect of water or electricity in certain cases have deprived Manipur and other Northeastern states of a major source of income, because of all these reasons in the country. The North East has the biggest potential for cheap production of hydro electric power which could earn many crores of rupees as profit if harnessed properly; (Art. 288, dealing with exemption from taxation by states in respect of water or electricity in certain cases).

(i) Save in so far as the President may order otherwise provided, no law of a state in force immediately before the commencement of this constitution shall impose or authorize the imposition of a tax in respect of any water or electricity stored, generated, consumed, distributed, or sold by any authority established by existing law or any law made by the parliament for regulating or developing any inter-state river or river valley.

(ii) The legislature of a state may by law impose, or authorize the imposition of any such tax as is mentioned in clause 1 but, no such law shall have any effect unless it has, after having been reserved for the consideration of the President, received his accent; and if any such law provides for the fixation of the rates and the other incidents of such tax by means of rules or orders to be made under the law by any authority, the law shall provide for the previous consent of the President being obtained to the making of any such rule or order.

Because of the above constitutional provisions, the government of Manipur cannot levy any tax directly on electrical energy generated by Loktak Hydro Electric Project without obtaining the assent of the President of India and therefore, the state has been deprived of a major share of the profit from this project. Unless this constitutional provisions are amended, the state will not be entitled to a share of the huge profit which is going to be earned from a number of hydro electric projects, which are going to be taken up in the state in the coming years. If the state has the power to levy taxes on electricity generated in the state by any authority or if power generation, is made purely a state subject, the state government will be able to earn many crores every year as net income or profit from the sale of electrical energy to other states or countries. If that is so, the government of Manipur will commission other major hydro-electric projects.

Colonial Understanding of Land needs to be Changed

The Government of India has decided to amend the Land Acquisition Act 1894 enacted by the British to acquire land for economic exploitation of the country. The independent Indian state took over the colonial law with its colonial understanding of land, lock, stock and barrel and carried on with it for the last 50 years. Under the garb of 'public purpose' the state went on acquiring the land of the poor and marginalised indiscriminately. As per colonial understanding, land was an economic commodity to be bought and sold for profit in the market. All lands belonged to the state, individuals were mere tenants of the state. The colonial state abrogated to itself an absolute right and power to acquire any extent of the land and displaced people if they had occupied the land since ages. And the post-colonial Indian state is no exception. Since independence, the Indian state has operated through the same legal and economic framework.

However, for the indigenous peoples, land is a source of identity, security, existence, subsistence and life. But it could not be meaningful even though the 'Land Acquisition (Amendment) Bill 1998' was passed in the Parliament. The basic philosophy of the bill, by and large, still remains colonial. Concerned citizens, who wish to challenge the legal provision of the bill, have to raise a simple question: 'Does the land belong to the eminent domain (state), public domain (communities,) or private domain?' In case the land belongs to the state, then the state has every right to acquire it from citizens who are mere tenants of the state. However, if the land belongs to the community, then the state has no locus standi to evolve a policy without community participation. What has to be contested by the indigenous peoples is the colonial understanding of land whereby the state still claims absolute ownership of land.

Removal of Black Laws

Another defect of both the Union Government and state government is that the genuine political problems and the acute social and political discontent have not been taken care of. Instead they are sought to be crushed. Sometimes it is done through the police, sometime with the help of Para-military forces and usually the army is directly used. Whatever be the details, the fact remains that the political problems are not solved politically; instead force is being used. People are really in trouble because of implementing the Armed Forces Special Power Act, 1958 and other black laws. People have been agitating for more than two decades to repeal such acts but all are in vain. Even Sharmila has been in hunger strike unto death for more than half a decade to repeal all these black laws. Today, count down for death is knocking at the door; however the governments at both the centre and the state are ignoring the non-violent methods.

State Boundary should not be altered by the Constitutions

The Boundary of Manipur state should not be altered by the Constitution's Articles 3 on the ground that it is a tiny state having an area of only 22,357 sq.km., out of which only one-tenth is the valley and remaining is the hill. How could the state of Manipur exist as a state after bifurcating a large portion of the land because territorial viability is the essential elements of the state. Moreover, it will hurt the symbiotic relationship between the hill and valley people. So such an article should be made unapplicable for this tiny states of India.

Right to Secede means Meaningful Democracy

Basically, democracy has two important characteristics. They are liberty and equality. Without these, no one could say that the political system is democracy. So far the political issues of the North East states are concerned, the amendment of the constitution is highly needed to incorporate a new provision in which the unit states should unite to the union voluntarily and granting right to secede to all the unit states. This is the real feature of democratic constitution. Even the communist country Russia has this provision after the adoption of Russian Constitution in 1975. It is not the question of harbouring anti-Indian feeling. By assessing the fact that if it is so, the Government will also take proper care of other states of the North East. They are completely neglected by the centre for more than 50 years since its independence. Moreover, uneven development of all should also be checked by the centre.

It is very difficult, for this purpose, to elect members of a new Constituent Assembly at this stage. But there is no reason why the present two houses of parliament, namely, the Lok Sabha and Rajya Sabha cannot come together with a view to re-examine for the amendment of the constitution to bring about necessary changes for ensuring democratic procress with common political aspirations in the country.

Creating of Autonomous Tribal Areas Under Six Schedule

As far as creating of autonomous Tribal areas under Sixth Schedule for hills of Manipur is concerned, views are divided between those who favour it and tose who doesn't. Most of the valley people stand against Sixth Schedule because of the apprehension of dismembering Manipur State due to the demand for Greater Nagaland or Southern Nagaland by the Naga Underground organization . Another group of people want to give Sixth Schedule to hill areas with a huge economic package on the conditions that - (i) both finance commission and election commission of this autonomy should be in the hands of state, (ii) Five members should be nominated from micro-minority, (iii) the state government should have the power to dissolve the council if they try to alter the existing boundary of Manipur, (iv) Sixth Schedule should be given to only two backward districts like Tamenglong and Chandel districts. Some scholars are of the opinion that, instead of having autonomous council, there should be bi-cameral legislature in the state. The house should be represented by one member of each ethnic group irrespective of its size and population including some nominated outstanding personalities of tribal in various fields.

Lastly, we may conclude by saying that the problems of the North East are confined to this region itself in one side and in another side with the Government of India. So the emerging conflict situation can be classified as internal and external conflicts. Internal conflicts are really manifestation of the principle of antagonistic contradiction. So it becomes spiral in character. We have identified that there is not a fair degree of relationship between nation-state and ethnicity. State represents a political entity, while ethnicity has been the direct product of conquest colonization and immigration. We may say in an easy way that the basis of ethnic strife in the North East is a complex geo-political and displacement over the centuries. For this region itself, solution can be brought by means of people to people dialogue in order to live together, grow together and develop together with the available resources. Besides this, their interest can also be accommodated with the help of constitutional protection. At the same time, in the national relationship the constitution should be modified or amended for giving accommodation to the various interests of the various groups as to understand the political aspirations of them. Otherwise, nothing can be turned into the positive and constructive way. In other words, the centre should give the proper answer to the people of the North East and to the remark they often make. "Delhi is very far from us, how do we change our position from this Benthic location".

INDEX

■■■